WRITING SKILLS SUCCESS

CON INSTRUCCIONES EN ESPAÑOL

Judith F. Olson
Translated by Héctor A. Canonge

LEARNINGEXPRESS

NEW YORK

Library of Congress Cataloging-in-Publication Data:
Olson, Judith F.
    Writing skills success: con instrucciones en español / by Judith Olson—1st ed.
        p. cm.
    ISBN 1-57685-380-2
        1. English language—Textbooks for foreign speakers—Spanish. 2. English
    language—Grammar—Problems, exercises, etc. 3. English language—Composition
    and exercises. I. Title.

    PE 1129.S8 O59 2001
    428.2'461—dc21   2001029631

Printed in the United States of America
9 8 7 6 5 4 3 2 1
First Edition

ISBN 1-57685-380-2

For more information or to place an order, contact LearningExpress at:
        900 Broadway
        Suite 604
        New York, NY 10003

Or visit us at:
        www.learnatest.com

Un importante aviso para nuestros lectores

Si usted se ha prestado este libro de una escuela biblioteca pública, por favor no marque el libro, use un cuaderno separado para escribir sus respuestas y para que otra gente pueda usar el mismo material. Gracias por su cooperación y por tomar en cuenta a otras personas.

CONTENIDO

CÓMO USAR ESTE LIBRO

Escribir es como pescar. La gente que sabe pescar bien lo ha estudiado y practicado. Ellos aprenden a usar diferentes herramientas para poder pescar el mejor pez en diferentes tipos de aguas. Nadie nace con el talento para pescar. Algunas personas lo disfrutan más que otras, pero casi todos lo pueden hacer si lo desea. Lo mismo se puede decir de la escritura.

Ya que usted compró este libro, usted probablemente quiere o necesita aprender más sobre el proceso de escribir y como llegar a ser un mejor escritor. Este libro le ayudará a adquirir el misterioso y reguardado poder de la pluma en las fáciles 20 lecciones que siguen. Este libro cubre lo básico de la escritura; puntuación, uso, dicción y organización. Usted no encontrará charlatanería en este libro ya que es para gente ocupada que quiere aprender lo más posible. Cada lección contiene suficientes ejemplos que le servirán de ejemplo, oportunidades para practicar las técnicas, y sugerencias para usarlas en su vida diaria.

Mucha gente tiene miedo de una hoja de papel en blanco o una pantalla vacía en la computadora. "No sé lo que voy a escribir. A pesar de saber lo que quiero decir, tengo miedo de decirlo incorrectamente o que suene como algo estúpido."

Pero eso es una de las cosas que uno tiene que amar a cerca de la escritura. El escribir es un proceso. La primera vez que usted escribe en un borrador, no importa si lo que ha escrito parezca incorrecto o suene como algo estúpido ya que usted puede cambiarlo cuantas veces lo desee. Usted puede revisar su borrador hasta que esté completamente satisfecho, o hasta que decida cambiar de dirección. Usted puede mostrar su borrador a sus amigos o familia y recibir una respuesta antes de hacerlo algo público.

No ponga demasiada presión en su persona pensando en que nunca podrá producir en un primer intento una obra perfecta. Nadie se puede sentar y escribir mensajes, reportes, o cartas pulidas sin tener que cambiar o revisar un poco. Inclusive los más profesionales tienen que revisar algo. Por ejemplo, el escritor Ernest Hemingway tuvo que revisar la última página de su famosa novela *A Farewell to Arms* treinta y nueve veces antes de estar satisfecho con la misma. Es más probable que usted no quiera revisar nada tantas veces antes de la copia final, pero incluso si usted escribe dos o tres borradores, no es el único que necesitará hacerlo.

El lenguaje escrito tiene tres ventajas a diferencia del lenguaje hablado:

1. En la escritura, uno puede dar marcha atrás. La palabra hablada, al contrario, no puede ser revisada. Una vez que usted hace verblamente una declaración, ésta llega a afectar a sus oyentes de una manera particular y no puede "dar marcha atrás" o arreglarla al punto de que la primera declaración es olvidada. Por otro lado, si usted escribe una declaración y, despues de mirarla, se dá cuenta que suena ofensiva o incorrecta, usted la puede revisar antes de dirigirla a sus lectores. El escribir es una manera cuidadosa y muy bien pensada de comunicarse.

2. La escritura hace que usted clarifique sus ideas. Si está teniendo problemas al escribir, muy a menudo se debe a que usted todavía no ha terminado de pensar. Muchas veces, el sólo hecho de sentarse a escribir cualquier cosa que esté en su mente le ayudará a descubrir y organizar lo que piensa.

3. Otra de las ventajas es la permanencia. Ideas presentadas de forma escrita tienen más peso que las ideas habladas. Adicionalmente, éstas pueden ser revisadas y referidas a su forma exacta y original. Ideas habladas se basan a veces en la memoria inexacta de otras personas.

La escritura no es otra cosa más que los pensamientos en el papel-pensamientos organizados y muy bien elaborados. Mucha gente se siente protectora de sus pensamientos y, por lo tanto, prefiere mantenerlos ocultos en sus cabezas. Quizás algunos pensamientos deben ser mantenidos en privado, pero muchas ideas y observasiones maravillosas nunca salen a la superficie debido a que sus creadores no quieren expresarlas. Este libro puede ayudarle a expresar sus ideas de una manera clara y gramáticamente correcta. Después de que usted aprenda a insertar correctamente las comas y los puntos y comas, a usar verbos para crear fuertes imágines en su escritura, y de las otras técnicas básicas que se enseñan en este libro, usted ganará confianza en su habilidad como escritor. Inclusive, podrá avanzar y adquirir técnicas de escritura más avanzadas y sofisticadas después de haber dominado los conceptos básicos. Hoy en día son más y más los trabajos que requieren algún tipo de escritura, por lo tanto las técnicas que aprenda en este libro serán usadas eficientemente.

Las lecciones de este libro han sido diseñadas para ser completadas en aproximadamente 20 minutos por sección. Si usted estudia una lección por cada día de la semana, usted puede finalizar el curso entero en aproximadamente un mes. Por otro lado, usted puede encontrar otro método que trabaje mejor para usted. De todos modos, usted verá qué logra progresar si completa por lo menos dos lecciones por semana. Si deja mucho tiempo entre lecciones, se olvidará de lo que acaba de aprender. Si quiere, puede empezar con la prueba evaluativa que comienza en la próxima página. Le demostrará lo que ya sabe y lo que necesita aprender sobre gramática, mecánicos, y puntuación. Después, cuando finalice el libro, puede tomar el examen final para ver cuanto ha logrado mejorar.

Si usted practica lo que ha aprendido en este libro, no tomará mucho tiempo en que la gente se dé cuenta de su progreso. Eso es lo que se logra mediante la práctica—ésta le ayuda a que uno mejore en cualquier cosa a la cual uno le está dedicando tiempo, ya sea pescando o escribiendo. Por lo tanto, comience con la primera lección de este libro y esté listo para mejorar su escritura. ¡Buena suerte!

PRUEBA DE EVALUACIÓN

Antes de empezar con el estudio de la gramática y las técnicas de escritura, usted puede tener una idea de lo que ya sabe y de cuanto más necesita aprender. Si éste es el caso, tome la siguiente prueba de evaluación.

Esta prueba evaluativa consiste en 50 preguntas multiples y cubren todas las lecciones de este libro. Naturalmente, 50 preguntas no pueden cubrir cada uno de los conceptos o reglas individuales que aprenderá estudiando este libro. Incluso si llegara a contestar correctamente todas las preguntas de esta prueba, le garantizamos que encontrará algunas ideas o reglas de las cuales usted no tenía conocimiento alguno. Por otro lado, si usted no llegase a contestar incorrectamente muchas de las preguntas, no se desespere. Este libro le mostrará paso a paso como obtener mejor gramática y escritura.

Por lo tanto, use esta prueba para tener una idea general de cuanto usted sabe de la materia presentada en este libro. Si obtiene un puntaje alto en esta prueba, puede que necesite dedicar al libro menos tiempo del originalmente planeado. Si obtiene un puntaje bajo, encontrará que quizás necesite más de 20 minutos diarios para cubrir cada capítulo y aprender toda la gramática y conceptos mecánicos que necesita.

Existe una página de respuestas que puede usar para apuntar sus respuestas en la siguiente página. Si usted prefiere, en este libro, marque sus respuestas dentro de un círculo. Si el libro no le pertenece, escriba los números del 1-50 en una hoja de papel aparte y apunte sus respuestas en ésta. Tome el tiempo necesario para tomar esta prueba sencilla. Una vez que termine, revise sus respuestas y compárelas con las respuestas claves que siguen la prueba. Cada respuesta indica la lección que le enseñará las reglas gramaticales que cubre la pregunta.

1.	a	b	c	d	21.	a	b	c	d	41.	a	b	c	d
2.	a	b	c	d	22.	a	b	c	d	42.	a	b	c	d
3.	a	b	c	d	23.	a	b	c	d	43.	a	b	c	d
4.	a	b	c	d	24.	a	b	c	d	44.	a	b	c	d
5.	a	b	c	d	25.	a	b	c	d	45.	a	b	c	d
6.	a	b	c	d	26.	a	b	c	d	46.	a	b	c	d
7.	a	b	c	d	27.	a	b	c	d	47.	a	b	c	d
8.	a	b	c	d	28.	a	b	c	d	48.	a	b	c	d
9.	a	b	c	d	29.	a	b	c	d	49.	a	b	c	d
10.	a	b	c	d	30.	a	b	c	d	50.	a	b	c	d
11.	a	b	c	d	31.	a	b	c	d					
12.	a	b	c	d	32.	a	b	c	d					
13.	a	b	c	d	33.	a	b	c	d					
14.	a	b	c	d	34.	a	b	c	d					
15.	a	b	c	d	35.	a	b	c	d					
16.	a	b	c	d	36.	a	b	c	d					
17.	a	b	c	d	37.	a	b	c	d					
18.	a	b	c	d	38.	a	b	c	d					
19.	a	b	c	d	39.	a	b	c	d					
20.	a	b	c	d	40.	a	b	c	d					

PRUEBA DE EVALUACIÓN

1. Which version of the sentence is correctly capitalized?
   a. Last Thursday, my Mother, my Aunt Sarah, and I went to the museum to see an exhibit of African art.
   b. Last Thursday, my mother, my Aunt Sarah, and I went to the museum to see an exhibit of African art.
   c. Last Thursday, my mother, my aunt Sarah, and I went to the Museum to see an exhibit of African art.
   d. Last thursday, my mother, my aunt Sarah, and I went to the museum to see an exhibit of African Art.

2. Which of the underlined words in the following sentence should be capitalized?

   The <u>governor</u> gave a speech at the <u>fourth</u> of July picnic, which was held at my <u>cousin's</u> farm five miles <u>east</u> of town.

   a. governor
   b. fourth
   c. cousin's
   d. east

3. Which of the underlined words in the following sentence should be capitalized?

   "Last <u>semester</u>, I wrote my <u>history</u> report on the Korean <u>war</u>," my <u>sister</u> told me.

   a. semester
   b. history
   c. war
   d. sister

4. Which version uses periods correctly?
   a. Dr Harrison will speak at a hotel in Chicago, Ill, on Thurs at 3:00 P.M.
   b. Dr. Harrison will speak at a hotel in Chicago, Ill, on Thurs at 3:00 PM.
   c. Dr Harrison will speak at a hotel in Chicago, Ill, on Thurs. at 3:00 P.M.
   d. Dr. Harrison will speak at a hotel in Chicago, Ill., on Thurs. at 3:00 P.M.

5. Which version uses punctuation correctly?
   a. Watch out. The road is icy?
   b. Watch out! The road is icy.
   c. Watch out? The road is icy!
   d. Watch out, the road is icy?

6. Which one is a sentence fragment, that is, NOT a complete sentence?
   a. Hearing the thunder, the lifeguard ordered us out of the water.
   b. Turn off the lights.
   c. Sunday afternoon spent reading and playing computer games.
   d. I was surprised to see that my neighbor had written a letter to the editor.

7. Three of the following sentences are faulty. They are either run-ons or comma splices. Which one is NOT a faulty sentence?
   a. The newspapers are supposed to be delivered by 7:00, but I am usually finished before 6:45.
   b. I called the delivery service this morning, they told me the shipment would arrive on time.
   c. Look in the closet you should find it there.
   d. I was the first to sign the petition Harry was second.

WRITING SKILLS SUCCESS CON INSTRUCCIONES EN ESPAÑOL

8. Which version is punctuated correctly?
   a. Charlotte, who ran in the Boston Marathon last year will compete in this year's New York Marathon.
   b. Charlotte who ran in the Boston Marathon, last year, will compete in this year's New York Marathon.
   c. Charlotte who ran in the Boston Marathon last year, will compete in this year's New York Marathon.
   d. Charlotte, who ran in the Boston Marathon last year, will compete in this year's New York Marathon.

9. Which version is punctuated correctly?
   a. The park service will not allow anyone, who does not have a camping permit, to use this campground.
   b. The park service will not allow anyone who does not have a camping permit to use this campground.
   c. The park service will not allow anyone, who does not have a camping permit to use this campground.
   d. The park service will not allow anyone who does not have a camping permit, to use this campground.

10. Which version is punctuated correctly?
   a. As soon as he finished his homework, Rod, who is a member of the baseball team, went to batting practice.
   b. As soon as he finished his homework Rod, who is a member of the baseball team went to batting practice.
   c. As soon as he finished, his homework, Rod who is a member of the baseball team, went to batting practice.
   d. As soon as he finished his homework, Rod who is a member of the baseball team went to batting practice.

11. Which of the underlined portions of the sentence below is punctuated INCORRECTLY?

My mother was born on (a) <u>December 15, 1944,</u> in Kingwood, West (b) <u>Virginia, when</u> she was (c) <u>five, her</u> family moved to (d) <u>347 Benton Street, Zanesville, Ohio.</u>

12. Which version is punctuated correctly?
   a. Yes I would like to see a copy of the report and please send it today by priority mail.
   b. Yes, I would like to see a copy of the report and please send it, today by priority mail.
   c. Yes, I would like to see a copy of the report and, please send it today by priority mail.
   d. Yes, I would like to see a copy of the report, and please send it today by priority mail.

13. Which version is punctuated correctly?
   a. I'm sorry, Bart, that you cannot meet us for dinner tonight. We'll phone you again next Friday.
   b. I'm sorry, Bart that you cannot meet us for dinner tonight. We'll phone you again next Friday.
   c. I'm sorry Bart that you cannot meet us for dinner tonight. We'll phone you again next Friday.
   d. I'm sorry, Bart, that you cannot meet us for dinner tonight, we'll phone you again next Friday.

4   *LearningExpress Skill Builders*

14. Which is the correct punctuation for the underlined portion?

    The weather forecasters are predicting ten inches of snow <u>tonight therefore</u> the annual chili supper will be rescheduled for next week.

    a. tonight, therefore
    b. tonight, therefore,
    c. tonight; therefore,
    d. tonight, therefore;

15. Which is the correct punctuation for the underlined portion?

    You may choose to read any two of the following <u>novels</u> *The Great Gatsby*, *Song of Solomon*, *Sophie's Choice*, *The Color Purple*, *The Bell Jar*, and *The Invisible Man*.

    a. novels, *The*
    b. novels: *The*
    c. novels; *the*
    d. novels. *The*

16. Which version is punctuated correctly?
    a. One of my concerns—if you really want to know is that the city council will vote against the new plan.
    b. One of my concerns—if you really want to know—is that the city council will vote against the new plan.
    c. One of my concerns, if you really want to know—is that the city council will vote against the new plan.
    d. One of my concerns if you really want to know is that the city council will vote against the new plan.

17. Which version is punctuated correctly?
    a. You will find boys' shirts in the childrens' department.
    b. You will find boy's shirts in the children's department.
    c. You will find boys' shirts in the children's department.
    d. You will find boy's shirts in the childrens' department.

18. Which version is punctuated correctly?
    a. Whose coat is this? Is it yours or Eric's?
    b. Whose coat is this? Is it your's or Eric's?
    c. Who's coat is this? Is it your's or Eric's?
    d. Who's coat is this? Is it yours or Eric's?

19. Which version is punctuated correctly?
    a. "May I ride with you?" asked Del. "I can't get my car started."
    b. May I ride with you? asked Del. "I can't get my car started."
    c. "May I ride with you? asked Del. I can't get my car started."
    d. "May I ride with you"? asked Del, "I can't get my car started."

20. Which of the following should be placed in quotation marks and should NOT be italicized or underlined?
    a. the name of a ship
    b. the title of a poem
    c. the title of a novel
    d. the name of a newspaper

21. Which version uses hyphens correctly?
a. The well-known singer-songwriter gave a three hour concert.
b. The well known singer songwriter gave a three-hour concert.
c. The well-known singer-songwriter gave a three-hour concert.
d. The well known singer-songwriter gave a three hour concert.

22. Which of the following should NOT be hyphenated?
a. twenty-one students
b. two-inch nails
c. a thirty-minute interview
d. ten-feet of rope

23. Which version uses parentheses correctly?
a. I plan to do my geography report on the Central American country of Belize (formerly known as British Honduras).
b. I plan to do my geography report on the (Central American country of) Belize, formerly known as British Honduras.
c. I plan to do my (geography) report on the Central American country of Belize, formerly known as British Honduras.
d. I plan to do my geography report on the Central American country (of Belize) formerly known as British Honduras.

Para contestar las preguntas 24 y 25, use la forma correcta del verbo.

24. Last night, Rita _____ a standing ovation for her performance.
a. has gotten
b. gotten
c. will get
d. got

25. Bart _____ cupcakes so we could all celebrate his birthday.
a. brang
b. brought
c. bring
d. had brung

26. Which of the following underlined verbs is NOT written in the correct tense?

Last week, we (a) <u>went</u> camping in Zion National Park. We (b) <u>hike</u> several hours each-day. At night, I (c) <u>climbed</u> into my sleeping bag exhausted, but in the morning I (d) <u>couldn't wait</u> to get started again.

27. Choose the version that correctly rewrites the following sentence in the active voice.

I was taken to the public library by my sister before I was able to read.
a. Before I was able to read, I was taken to the public library by my sister.
b. Before learning to read, my sister took me to the public library.
c. Before I was able to read, my sister took me to the public library.
d. I was taken to the public library before I knew how to read, by my sister.

28. Which of the following sentences is in the passive voice?
a. On Saturday nights, we made popcorn.
b. Our bowls were filled and brought into the living room.
c. We sat on the floor and watched the movie we had rented.
d. One of us usually fell asleep before the movie was over.

Para contestar las preguntas 29 y 30, elija el verbo que concuerda con el tema de la oración.

29. Neither of the dogs _____ to obedience training.
a. have been
b. were
c. is been
d. has been

30. The art professor, along with several of her students, _____ to attend the gallery opening tomorrow evening.
a. is planning
b. are planning
c. plan
d. have planned

31. Choose the subject that agrees with the verb in the following sentence.

_____ of the customers have complained about poor service.

a. One
b. Neither
c. Each
d. Some

32. In which of the following sentences is the underlined verb NOT in agreement with the subject of the sentence?

a. Where <u>are</u> the forms you want me to fill out?
b. Which <u>is</u> the correct form?
c. Here <u>is</u> the forms you need to complete.
d. There <u>are</u> two people who still need to complete the form.

33. In which of the following sentences is the underlined pronoun INCORRECT?
a. Alicia and <u>me</u> want to spend Saturday at Six Flags Amusement Park.
b. Either Sam or William will bring <u>his</u> CD player to the party.
c. She and <u>I</u> will work together on the project.
d. Why won't you let <u>her</u> come with us?

34. In which of the following sentences is the underlined pronoun INCORRECT?
a. Francine can run much faster than <u>me.</u>
b. Erin and Bob are painting the house <u>themselves.</u>
c. Five members of the team and <u>I</u> will represent our school.
d. Our neighbors gave <u>us</u> some tomatoes from their garden.

Para contestar las preguntas 35-38, elija una de las opciones que mejor complete la oración.

35. Four band members and _____ were chosen to attend the state competition. One of _____ will do the driving.
a. me, we
b. me, us
c. I, we
d. I, us

36. Marcus _____ the bags of groceries on the kitchen table fifteen minutes ago.
a. had sat
b. set
c. sit
d. sat

37. About five minutes after the sun _____, my
alarm goes off, and _____ time to get up.
a. raises, it's
b. raises, its
c. rises, it's
d. rises, its

38. Paula did _____ on the test, but Georgia
had the _____ score in the class.
a. good, better
b. good, best
c. well, better
d. well, best

39. Which of the sentences is clearly and correctly
written?
a. Driving along the country road, a deer ran in
front of us.
b. A deer ran in front of us while driving along
the country road.
c. As we were driving along the country road, a
deer ran in front of us.
d. Running in front of us, we saw the deer, driving along the country road.

Para contestar las preguntas 40-46, elija una
de las opciones que complete la oración
correctamente.

40. If we divide this pizza _____ the five people here, there won't be _____ pieces left over.
a. among, any
b. among, no
c. between, any
d. between, no

41. Yesterday, I _____ the campers to the _____
we had chosen near the river.
a. lead, cite
b. lead, site
c. led, cite
d. led, site

42. As we have done in the _____, we will
_____ at the coffee house at 10:00 A.M.
a. past, meet
b. past, meat
c. passed, meet
d. passed, meat

43. As you can _____ see, there has been a
_____ in the water pipe.
a. planely, brake
b. planely, break
c. plainly, brake
d. plainly, break

44. Do you know _____ Teresa will
_____ to join our organization?
a. weather, choose
b. weather, chose
c. whether, choose
d. whether, chose

45. _____ are the magazines that _____ to be
stacked on this table?
a. Wear, used
b. Wear, use
c. Where, used
d. Where, use

46. Do you _____ if the Giants _____ the game?
   a. know, one
   b. know, won
   c. no, one
   d. no, won

47. Which of the following phrases contains a redundancy; that is, it repeats words that express the same idea?
   a. I did not hear the phone ring.
   b. You always perform your job efficiently.
   c. The umpire has temporarily suspended the game until later.
   d. Jenna and Erin have both contributed greatly to our team's success.

48. Which of the following sentences contains a cliché?
   a. The room was so quiet, you could hear a pin drop.
   b. Your plan is not in accordance with the regulations set down by the review board.
   c. The stars were pinpricks in the tarpaper sky.
   d. Due to the fact that it snowed, the trip was canceled.

49. Which version has a consistent point of view?
   a. The history of English is divided into three periods. You could mark the earliest one at about the fifth century A.D.
   b. You can say that the history of English could be divided into three periods, and I know the earliest one begins about the fifth century A.D.
   c. The history of English is divided into three periods. The earliest one begins at about the fifth century A.D.
   d. I learned that the history of English is divided into three periods and that you begin the earliest one at about the fifth century A.D.

50. Which version has a parallel structure?
   a. We write for a variety of purposes: in expressing our feelings, to convey information, to persuade, or to give pleasure.
   b. We write for a variety of purposes: to express our feelings, convey information, persuasion, or giving pleasure.
   c. We write for a variety of purposes: an expression of our feelings, conveying information, persuade, or to give pleasure.
   d. We write for a variety of purposes: to express our feelings, to convey information, to persuade, or to give pleasure.

LISTA DE RESPUESTAS

Si respondió a alguna pregunta incorrectamente, usted puede encontrar ayuda para resolver ese tipo de pregunta en la lección enumerada al lado derecho de la respuesta correcta.

1. b. Lección 1
2. b. Lección 1
3. c. Lección 1
4. d. Lección 2
5. b. Lección 2
6. c. Lección 3
7. a. Lección 3
8. d. Lección 4
9. b. Lección 4
10. a. Lección 4
11. b. Lecciones 5, 6
12. d. Lección 5
13. a. Lección 5
14. c. Lección 6
15. b. Lección 6
16. b. Lección 7
17. c. Lección 7
18. a. Lección 7
19. a. Lección 8
20. b. Lección 8
21. c. Lección 9
22. d. Lección 9
23. a. Lección 9
24. d. Lección 10
25. b. Lección 10

26. b. Lección 10
27. c. Lección 11
28. b. Lección 11
29. d. Lección 12
30. a. Lección 12
31. d. Lección 12
32. c. Lección 12
33. a. Lección 13
34. a. Lección 13
35. d. Lección 13
36. b. Lección 14
37. c. Lección 14
38. d. Lección 14
39. c. Lección 15
40. a. Lección 15
41. d. Lección 16
42. a. Lección 16
43. d. Lección 16
44. c. Lección 17
45. c. Lección 17
46. b. Lección 17
47. c. Lección 18
48. a. Lección 18
49. c. Lección 19
50. d. Lección 19

USO DE MAYÚSCULAS

1

RESUMEN DE LA LECCIÓN

Hoy aprenderá sobre los detalles más importantes en el uso de mayúsculas. El capítulo divide el uso de mayúsculas en dos categorías: reglas generales que gobiernan el uso de mayúsculas y reglas específicas relacionadas con los nombres propios y los adjetivos.

Empiece por ver cuánto yá sabe sobre el uso correcto de las letras mayúsculas. En la próxima página el mismo párrafo ha sido escrito dos veces. La primera columna, llamada **Problema**, no contiene ninguna mayúscula—en definitiva un problema de escritura! Encierre en un círculo esas letras del **Problema** que usted cree deben ser mayúsculas, y luego verifique usted mismo en la columna de **Solución**.

Problema

when I first saw the black hills on january 2, 1995, i was shocked by their beauty. we had just spent new year's day in sioux falls, south dakota, and had headed west toward our home in denver, colorado. as we traveled along interstate 90, i could see the black hills rising slightly in the distance. after driving through the badlands and stopping at wall drug in wall, south dakota, the evergreen-covered hills broke the barren monotony of the landscape. my oldest daughter said, "dad, look! there's something that's not all white." we saw mount rushmore and custer state park, the home of the largest herd of buffalo in north america. we also drove the treacherous spearfish canyon road. fortunately, our jeep cherokee had no trouble with the ice and snow on the winding road. we were unable to see needles national park because the needles highway was snowed shut. winter may not be the best time to see these sights, but we enjoyed them nonetheless.

Solución

When I first saw the Black Hills on January 2, 1995, I was shocked by their beauty. We had just spent New Year's Day in Sioux Falls, South Dakota, and had headed west toward our home in Denver, Colorado. As we traveled along Interstate 90, I could see the Black Hills rising slightly in the distance. After driving through the Badlands and stopping at Wall Drug in Wall, South Dakota, the evergreen-covered hills broke the barren monotony of the landscape. My oldest daughter said, "Dad, look! There's something that's not all white." We saw Mount Rushmore and Custer State Park, the home of the largest herd of buffalo in North America. We also drove the treacherous Spearfish Canyon Road. Fortunately, our Jeep Cherokee had no trouble with the ice and snow on the winding road. We were unable to see Needles National Park because the Needles Highway was snowed shut. Winter may not be the best time to see these sights, but we enjoyed them nonetheless.

¿Cómo lo hizo? A medida que usted avance la lección, trate de identificar las reglas específicas que usted no aplicó correctamente.

REGLAS GENERALES DEL USO DE MAYÚSCULAS

La tabla que sigue resume el uso general de las mayúsculas. Las reglas que tienen que ver con categorias especí-ficas de los nombre propios se verán en el capítulo que sigue.

REGLAS DEL USO DE MAYÚSCULAS	
Regla	**Ejemplo**
Ponga una mayúscula en la primera palabra de una oración. Si la primera palabra es un número, escríbalo en palabras.	This is the first word of the sentence. Three of us worked the early shift.
El pronombre *I* o la contracción *I'm* siempre se escribe en mayúscula, y tambien las abreviaciones *B.C.* o *A.D.*	The group left when **I** asked them to go. The manuscript was dated 501 **A.D.**
Use mayúsculas en la primera palabra de una cita. La primera palabra de una cita incompleta no debe ser escrita en mayúscula.	I said, "**W**hat's the name of your dog?" He called me "the worst excuse for a student" he had ever seen.

Abajo le damos el ejemplo de un diálogo que demuestra las reglas, anteriormente expuestas. (Una nota sobre el uso de párrafos en un diálogo: cada vez que el que habla termina de hacerlo, comience un nuevo párrafo.)

"**G**ood morning," said the new supervisor as **I** entered the door.

"**G**ood morning!" **I** answered, somewhat surprised. "**Y**ou must be Ms. Barnes. **I**'m Joshua Haines. **I**t's a plea-sure to meet you."

"**T**ell me what you do, Joshua. **I**'m anxious to learn all about this operation."

I smiled and said, "**T**hat doesn't surprise me. **I** heard you were a '**s**ieve for information.'"

PRÁCTICA

Compruebe su habilidad de aplicar las reglas anteriormente mencionadas. De cada uno de los siguientes grupos, elija la opción correcta que incluye el uso de mayúsculas. Las respuestas para cada grupo de preguntas pueden ser encontradas al final de la lección.

1. a. the memo confused me at first. after a few readings i was able to understand it.
   b. The memo confused me at first. after a few readings I was able to understand it.
   c. The memo confused me at first. After a few readings I was able to understand it.

2. a. "where are you going?" my coworker asked.
      "to a meeting i'm not very excited about," i answered.
   b. "Where are you going?" my coworker asked.
      "To a meeting I'm not very excited about," I answered.

    c. "Where are you going?" My coworker asked

       "To a meeting I'm not very excited about," I answered.

3. a. we read the poem written in 1493 A.D

    b. We read the poem written in 1493 a.d.

    c. We read the poem written in 1493 A.D.

4. a. When you return from your trip, I want a full report of your activities.

    b. when you return from your trip, I want a full report of your activities.

    c. When you return from your trip, i want a full report of your activities.

NOMBRES Y ADJETIVOS PROPIOS

Todos los nombres y adjetivos propios—esos que nominan específicamente a una persona, lugar o cosa—tienen que ser escritos en mayúsculas, pero el recordar cuáles de ellos realmente lo son es un tanto dificultoso. La tabla que sigue incluye las caractéristicas más comunes de los nombre y adjetivos propios. Cada sección comienza con una tabla que muestra 5-7 reglas relacionadas, seguidas por varios ejercicios de práctica.

NOMBRES PROPIOS, PRIMERA PARTE	
Categoría de Nombre Propio	**Ejemplo**
Días de la semana	Friday, Saturday
Meses	January, February
Días feriados	Christmas, Halloween
Eventos y periodos históricos, documentos	Civil War (historical event), Dark Ages (historical period), Declaration of Independence (document)
Eventos especiales, eventos del calendario	Pebble Beach Fall Classic, Renaissance Festival, Green River Days (special events); Labor Day, Father's Day (calendar events)
Nombres de personas y lugares	John Doe, Lincoln Center, Sears Tower

PRÁCTICA

Usando las reglas anteriores, elija la versión correcta de mayúsculas de los siguientes pares de oraciones.

5. a. Chaucer was one of the foremost poets from the Middle ages.

    b. Chaucer was one of the foremost poets from the Middle Ages.

6. a. The Olsons spend Labor Day and four weeks of each summer at their lakeside cottage.

    b. The Olsons spend Labor day and four weeks of each Summer at their Lakeside cottage.

7. a. We studied the declaration of independence in History class.

b. We studied the Declaration of Independence in history class.

8. a. Judy has two Uncles who fought in world war II.

b. Judy has two uncles who fought in World War II.

NOMBRES PROPIOS, SEGUNDA PARTE

Categoría de Nombre Propio	Ejemplos
Nombres de estructuras y edificios	Washington Memorial, Empire State Building
Nombres de trenes, barcos, aviones, y otros medios de transporte	Queen Elizabeth, Discovery, Sioux Lines, TransWorld Airlines
Nombres de productos	Corn King hams, Dodge Intrepid
Nombres de cargos oficiales	Mayor Daley, President Clinton
Trabajos de arte y literatura	*Black Elk Speaks* (book), "Mending Wall" (poem), Mona Lisa (painting)
Grupos étnicos, razas, lenguajes, nacionalidades	Asian-American, Caucasian, French, Indian

PRÁCTICA

De cada uno de los siguientes pares elija la versión correcta del uso de mayúsculas.

9. a. I enjoyed *spoon river anthology* by Edgar Lee Masters.

b. I enjoyed *Spoon River Anthology* by Edgar Lee Masters.

10. a. We caught a Vanguard Airlines flight to Orlando.

b. We caught a Vanguard airlines flight to Orlando.

11. a. The Talmud is a guide to the teachings of judaism.

b. The Talmud is a guide to the teachings of Judaism.

12. a. Paul has an editing job with Meredith publishing.

b. Paul has an Editing job with Meredith Publishing.

13. a. The university of iowa has an outstanding Law School.

b. The University of Iowa has an outstanding law school.

14. a. Dr. Gallagher researched her book at the Library of Congress.

b. Dr. Gallagher researched her book at the Library of congress.

NOMBRES PROPIOS, TERCERA PARTE

Categoría de Nombre Propio	Ejemplos
Ciudades, estados, y unidades gubernamentales	Des Moines, Iowa; Barrow, Alaska; Republic of South Africa
Calles, autopistas, y caminos	Grand Avenue, Interstate 29, Deadwood Road
Lugares reconocidos y regiones geográficas	Continental Divide, Grand Canyon
Áreas públicas y cuerpos de agua	Superior Forest, Missouri River
Instituciones, organizaciones, y negocios	Dartmouth College, Lions Club, Dodge Trucks

PRÁCTICA

De cada uno de los siguientes pares elija la versión correcta del uso de mayúsculas.

15. a. In Switzerland, some citizens speak French, and others speak German.
   b. In switzerland, some citizens speak french, and others speak german.

16. a. Near a body of water called firth and forth, you can see Edinburgh, Scotland.
   b. Near a body of water called Firth and Forth, you can see Edinburgh, Scotland.

17. a. We drove along the Mississippi river to New Orleans.
   b. We drove along the Mississippi River to New Orleans.

18. a. Mount Everest, which is in the middle of the Himalayan Range, is the highest mountain in the world.
   b. Mount Everest, which is in the middle of the Himalayan Range, is the highest mountain in the World.

19. a. I have traveled on the Garden state Parkway, a main highway in New Jersey.
   b. I have traveled on the Garden State Parkway, a main highway in New Jersey.

ADJETIVOS PROPIOS

Los adjetivos propios son adjetivos—es decir, palabras que modifican al sustantivo-formados de un nombre propio, generalmente el nombre de un lugar. Por ejemplo, el nombre propio *Canada* se transforma en el adjetivo propio *Canadian* cuando modifica a otro sustantivo, como en *Canadian bacon*. Note que el nombre no está en mayúscula a no ser que sea un nombre propio en toda su legalidad.

Ejemplos:
English muffin, Polish sausage, Japanese yen

PRÁCTICA

De cada uno de los siguientes pares elija la versión correcta del uso de mayúsculas.

20. a. Some residents of ireland still speak the Gaelic Language.
   b. Some residents of Ireland still speak the Gaelic language.

21. a. Cortez, a Spanish explorer, conquered the Aztecs.

b. Cortez, a spanish explorer, conquered the Aztecs.

22. a. The actress in the play tried to speak with a Scottish accent.

b. The Actress in the play tried to speak with a Scottish accent.

23. a. I will never attempt to swim the English channel.

b. I will never attempt to swim the English Channel.

24. a. I had never been to a Sri Lankan Restaurant before.

b. I had never been to a Sri Lankan restaurant before.

CUANDO NO SE DEBE USAR MAYÚSCULAS

El escribir mayúsculas en palabras que no las necesiten es tan malo como no hacerlo con palabras que sí requieren de éstas. Tenga cuidado con estas trampas cuando se usan mayúsculas.

- Evada el uso innecesario de mayúsculas con los puntos cardinales; sin embargo, palabras que se refieren a un área específica de un país deben ser escritas en mayúsculas.

  Ejemplos:

  We headed **w**est after the Depression.

  The future of the country was cultivated in the **W**est.

- Evada el uso innecesario de mayúsculas al referirse a miembros familiares. Escríbalos en mayúsculas sólo cuando son usados como nombres. Si un pronombre posesivo (*my, our, your, his, her, their*) está escrito antes del nombre que refiere a un miembro familiar, éste no se debe escribir en mayúsculas.

  Ejemplos:

  When **U**ncle Harry visited last winter, none of my other **u**ncles came to see him.

  After my **m**other called me for lunch, **F**ather served the entree.

- Evada el uso innecesario de mayúsculas en estaciones del año o partes del año escolar.

  Ejemplo:

  If the university offers History of Education 405 in the **s**pring **s**emester, Horace will be able to graduate in
    May.

- Evada el uso innecesario de mayúsculas en disciplinas de estudio. Éstas sólo se escriben en mayúsculas si es que son parte del nombre de un curso específico.

  Ejemplos:

  I try to avoid **m**ath courses because I'm not very good at them.

  Betsy is taking **A**lgebra II and **T**rigonometry I next semester.

- Evada el uso innecesario de mayúsculas que estén modificadas por adjetivos propios.

    Ejemplos:

    Polish **s**ausage, not Polish Sausage

    Mexican **r**estaurant, not Mexican Restaurant

PRÁCTICA

De cada uno de los siguientes pares elija la versión correcta del uso de mayúsculas.

25. a. Digging the Canal through Panama took many years.

b. Digging the canal through Panama took many years.

26. a. The Smoky Mountains are in the Southeastern part of the country.

b. The Smoky Mountains are in the southeastern part of the country.

27. a. Nicholi Milani does more business in the East than in the West.

b. Nicholi Milani does more business in the east than in the west.

28. a. The Midwest had the coldest winter on record in 1993.

b. The midwest had the coldest winter on record in 1993.

29. a. Marianne had never been as far East as Columbus, Ohio.

b. Marianne had never been as far east as Columbus, Ohio.

Técnicas de aprendizaje

Lea un artículo del periódico local. Examine el uso de mayúsculas en el mismo. ¿Cuántas de las reglas que usted aprendió hoy fueron usadas en dicho artículo?

RESPUESTAS

1. c.	**9.** b.	**17.** b.	**25.** b.
2. b.	**10.** a.	**18.** a.	**26.** b.
3. c.	**11.** b.	**19.** b.	**27.** a.
4. a.	**12.** a.	**20.** b.	**28.** a.
5. b.	**13.** b.	**21.** a.	**29.** b.
6. a.	**14.** a.	**22.** a.	
7. b.	**15.** a.	**23.** b.	
8. b.	**16.** b.	**24.** b.	

L · E · C · C · I · Ó · N

PUNTUACIÓN

2

RESUMEN DE LA LECCIÓN

Esta lección le enseñará qué clases de puntuación se usan para finalizar oraciones. Las mismas son generalmente conocidas como "marcas finales." También le mostrará las otras maneras en que se usan los puntos finales.

E
l próximo ejercicio revisa Lección 1, El Uso de Mayúsculas, y le da una oportunidad para ver lo que ya sabe sobre los puntos finales y sobre las "marcas finales." Corrija el uso de mayúsculas en la columna **Problema** de la siguiente página añadiendo los puntos finales, signos de interrogación y exclamación, donde usted cree que son necesarios. A medida que avance, revise sus respuestas con la columna **Solución**.

Problema

The supervisors at Meredith industrial thought Henry Simmons, jr. was a less than Ideal employee if he was at work on monday, He would most likely be absent on Tuesday, and he had an annoying habit of extending his Holidays, such as christmas and thanksgiving, a few extra days so he could rest from all the activities What a problem he was

during one particular holiday, he had traveled East to be with his family he called his supervisor on the Day he was to return to work and explained that the Flight Schedule at the Airport had been altered and that he would not be able to catch another flight that he could afford until the weekend (Three days away) what do you suppose happened His supervisor suggested that he rent a car and drive the 600 miles from williamsborough, pennsylvania, to centerville, ohio he said that the drive would be less expensive than a Plane Fare and that henry might be able to save his job if he were only one day late, rather than three

Henry decided to try the suggested plan he went to budget rental on Main street in williamsborough and rented a Ford tempo for the trip being a literary person, he also stopped at Banoff's bookstore to buy a Book on Tape by Garrison keillor called *the book of guys* listening to it was a Life-Altering Experience for henry because it taught him all the things his Father had forgotten to mention

Solución

The supervisors at Meredith Industrial thought Henry Simmons, Jr., was a less than ideal employee. If he was at work on Monday, he would most likely be absent on Tuesday, and he had an annoying habit of extending his holidays, such as Christmas and Thanksgiving, a few extra days so he could rest from all the activities. What a problem he was!

During one particular holiday, he had traveled east to be with his family. He called his supervisor on the day he was to return to work and explained that the flight schedule at the airport had been altered and that he would not be able to catch another flight that he could afford until the weekend (three days away). What do you suppose happened? His supervisor suggested that he rent a car and drive the 600 miles from Williamsborough, Pennsylvania, to Centerville, Ohio. He said that the drive would be less expensive than a plane fare and that Henry might be able to save his job if he were only one day late, rather than three.

Henry decided to try the suggested plan. He went to Budget Rental on Main Street in Williamsborough and rented a Ford Tempo for the trip. Being a literary person, he also stopped at Banoff's Bookstore to buy a book on tape by Garrison Keillor called *The Book of Guys.* Listening to it was a life-altering experience for Henry because it taught him all the things his father had forgotten to mention

(Continua en la próxima página)

Problema (continuación)

before henry became a man can you imagine that

In fact, henry was so inspired that he decided to pursue a Degree in philosophy at centerville community college he enrolled in history of Philosophy 203 during the Spring Semester by the end of may, henry was hooked on Education and has not missed a class nor a Day of Work since

Solución (continuación)

before Henry became a man. Can you imagine that?

In fact, Henry was so inspired that he decided to pursue a degree in philosophy at Centerville Community College. He enrolled in History of Philosophy 203 during the spring semester. By the end of May, Henry was hooked on education and has not missed a class nor a day of work since.

REGLAS PARA EL USO DE PUNTO FINAL

- Use el punto final después de una inicial y después de cada parte de una abreviación, a no ser que ésta se haya transformado en un abreviación—como por ejemplo SIDA—o un nombre mundialmente reconocido (TV, FBI, CIA, NASA). Títulos—Mr., Ms., Dr., y más—son también abreviaciones que llevan punto aparte. Si la abreviación está al final de una oración, sólo un punto aparte es necesario.

  Ejemplos:

  The tour leaves on **Mon., Jan.** 1, at 3 P.M.

  The book was written by **C. S.** Lewis.

  A. J. Mandelli researched brain function for the **FBI.**

- Use el punto final antes de un decimal y entre dólares y centavos.

  Ejemplos:

  A gallon equals **3.875** liters.

  The new textbook costs **$54.75.**

  Only **5.6** percent of our consumers spend over **$100.00** per month on our products.

- Use el punto final al final de una oración declarativa.

  Ejemplos:

  Henry Kissinger served under two U. S. presidents.

  Wilson will lecture in the forum after school today.

  Many consider P. T. Barnum the best salesman ever to have walked the earth.

- Use el punto final al final de una oración que hace una petición, dá una instrucción, o declara algo.

  Ejemplos:

  Empty the kitchen trash before you take the garbage out.

  Turn right at the first stop light, and then go to the second house on the left.

- Use el punto final al final de una oración que hace una pregunta indirecta.
  Ejemplos:
  My neighbor asked if we had seen his cat. (The direct question was, "Have you seen my cat?")
  Quentin wanted to know how we had arrived at that answer. (The direct question was, "How did you arrive at that answer?")

PRÁCTICA

Elija la versión escrita correctamente de cada una de las siguientes oraciones. Usted encontrará las respuestas para cada grupo de preguntas al final de la lección.

1. a. The train passed through Rockford, Ill., on its way to St. Joseph, Mo.
b. The train passed through Rockford, Ill, on its way to St Joseph, Mo.
c. The train passed through Rockford, Ill, on its way to St. Joseph, Mo.

2. a. Ms Cory Ames, Dr Matthew Olson, and H. J. Lane went to Chicago, Ill..
b. Ms Cory Ames, Dr Matthew Olson, and HJ Lane went to Chicago, Ill.
c. Ms. Cory Ames, Dr. Matthew Olson, and H. J. Lane went to Chicago, Ill.

3. a. The bedrooms measured 12 ft. by 14 ft.
b. The bedrooms measured 12 ft by 14 ft.
c. The bedrooms measured 12 ft. by 14 ft..

4. a. Bob asked if the price of the CD was $13.98?
b. Bob asked if the price of the CD was $13.98.
c. Bob asked if the price of the CD was $1398¢.

5. a. Tie your shoe. Before you trip and break a leg.
b. Tie your shoe before you trip and break a leg.
c. Tie your shoe before you trip and break a leg

6. a. Mr and Mrs Fletcher visited 10 cities in 20 days.
b. Mr. and Mrs. Fletcher visited 10 cities in 20 days.
c. Mr and Mrs. Fletcher visited 10 cities in 20 days.

7. a. Mayor and Mrs. Dorian will address the city council at 8:00 PM
b. Mayor and Mrs Dorian will address the city council at 8:00 P.M.
c. Mayor and Mrs. Dorian will address the city council at 8:00 P.M.

8. a. Oh, all right. Tell me your riddle.
b. Oh. all right. Tell me your riddle.
c. Oh, all right Tell me your riddle.

REGLAS PARA USAR SIGNOS DE INTERROGACIÓN Y EXCLAMACIÓN

- Use el signo de interrogación después de una palabra o después de un grupo de palabras que hace una pregunta aun si no forma una oración completa.
  Ejemplos:
  What did you do last night?
  Will you put out the trash?
  Okay?

May we go to the movies after we've finished our homework?

Are we?

- Use el signo de exclamación después de una oración que expresa un sentimiento fuerte.

Ejemplos:

Look out for that car!

I just can't stand the smell in here!

Una palabra de advertencia sobre los signos de exclamación: Signos de exclamación son un poco como la sal en la comida. A la mayor parte de la gente les gusta un poco. A nadie le gusta en exceso.

- Use un signo de admiración después de una interjección—una palabra o frase que expresa un sentimiento muy fuerte—cuando está escrita como oración independiente y única.

Ejemplos:

Doggone it!

Yikes!

- Use un signo de admiración después de una oración que comience con una palabra interrogativa pero que no es una pregunta.

Ejemplos:

What a dunce I am!

How marvelous of you to come!

PRÁCTICA

De cada uno de los siguientes grupos elija la versión correcta.

9. a. Help! I'm falling?
b. Help! I'm falling.
c. Help! I'm falling!

10. a. I can't believe how naive I was!
b. I can't believe how naive I was.
c. I can't believe how naive I was?

11. a. The auditor asked me why I didn't save the receipts?
b. The auditor asked me why I didn't save the receipts.
c. The auditor asked me why I didn't save the receipts!

12. a. Can you tell me the seating capacity of this meeting room.
b. Can you tell me the seating capacity of this meeting room?
c. Can you tell me the seating capacity of this meeting room!

13. a. How utterly disgusting this movie is.
b. How utterly disgusting this movie is?
c. How utterly disgusting this movie is!

14. a. Was Alexander the Great born in 350 B.C.
b. Was Alexander the great born in 350 B.C.?
c. Was Alexander the Great born in 350 B.C.?

15. a. Our group will meet at the library at 10:00
P.M. to research T. S. Eliot.
b. Our group will meet at the library at 10:00
PM to research T. S. Eliot.
c. Our group will meet at the library at 10:00
P.M. to research TS. Eliot.

16. a. Is this sweater $59.95 or $69.95?
b. Is this sweater $59.95 or $69.95.
c. Is this sweater $5995 or $6995?

17. a. Wow. What a close call that was?
b. Wow! What a close call that was.
c. Wow! What a close call that was!

18. a. Those carpenters. Do you know how much
they charged?
b. Those carpenters? Do you know how much
they charged?
c. Those carpenters! Do you know how much
they charged?

Técnicas de aprendizaje

Tome algunos minutos para practicar lo que ha aprendido el día de hoy. Si usted está leyendo un libro ahora, ojee algunas páginas hasta que encuentre por lo menos tres ejemplos de cada una de las marcas finales que aprendió hoy. ¿Son usadas las marcas finales de acuerdo con las reglas? Si no está leyendo ningún libro, saque uno de los estantes en casa o en la oficina.

RESPUESTAS

1. a.
2. c.
3. a.
4. b.
5. b.

6. b.
7. c.
8. a.
9. c.
10. a.

11. b.
12. b.
13. c.
14. c.
15. a.

16. a.
17. c.
18. c.

3

EVADIENDO ORACIONES INCORRECTAS

RESUMEN DE LA LECCIÓN

Esta lección le ayudará a distinguir entre oraciones completas e incorrectas. De esa manera usted podrá evadir escribir fragmentos de oraciones, oraciones sin puntuación, y oraciones con el uso incorrecto de comas.

Comience su estudio de oraciones completas observando el párrafo **Problema** que aparece en la próxima página. Subraye los grupos de palabras que forman oraciones completas. Vea si usted puede distinguirlos de los fragmentos, las oraciones largas y las divisiones de comas incluidos en el párrafo. Entonces, revise su trabajo y compárelo con el párrafo **Solución** en la próxima página, donde las oraciones completas han sido subrayadas.

Problema

Just the other day I came home from work as excited as I had ever been. The night before someone from Publisher's Clearinghouse had called. To tell me that I would be receiving a prize package worth potentially millions of dollars. I was so excited because, unlike other offers, this really sounded legitimate, it sounded to me as though I might really win something this time. I hastily opened the mailbox. Hoping to find the promised envelope. There it was. Between the *Life* magazine and the Fingerhut catalog. The promised letter. When I finally finished reading the entire mailing. I realized my chances were really no better with this contest than they had been for any other contest I had entered in the past and I was disappointed that I had spent so much time reading all of the material then I threw it all in the recycling basket and went to bed. Dejected.

Solución

<u>Just the other day I came home from work as excited as I had ever been.</u> <u>The night before someone from Publisher's Clearinghouse had called.</u> To tell me that I would be receiving a prize package worth potentially millions of dollars. I was so excited because, unlike other offers, this really sounded legitimate, it sounded to me as though I might really win something this time. <u>I hastily opened the mailbox.</u> Hoping to find the promised envelope. <u>There it was.</u> Between the *Life* magazine and the Fingerhut catalog. The promised letter. When I finally finished reading the entire mailing. I realized my chances were really no better with this contest than they had been for any other contest I had entered in the past and I was disappointed that I had spent so much time reading all of the material then I threw it all in the recycling basket and went to bed. Dejected.

ORACIONES COMPLETAS

Una oración completa es un grupo de palabras que cumple los tres siguientes requisitos:

1. Tiene un verbo (una palabra o frase que explica una determinada acción como por ejemplo *want, run, take, give,* o una condición de ser como por ejemplo: *am, is, are, was, were, be.* Muchas oraciones tienen más de un solo verbo. Los verbos en la oración que sigue han sido marcados para usted.

Ejemplos:
   Bob and Alexandra both **want** a promotion. (acción verbal)
   Yurika **drafted** a memo and **sent** it to the sales department. (acción verbal)
   Herbert and Tan **are** the chief operators in this department. (condición verbal)

2. Tiene un sujeto (alguien o algo que lleva a cabo la acción o sirve como foco principal de la oración). Así como los verbos, muchas oraciones también tienen más de un sujeto.

Ejemplos:

Bob and **Alexandra** both want a promotion.

Yurika drafted a memo and sent it to the sales department.

Herbert and **Tan** are the chief operators in this department.

3. Comunica un pensamiento completo. Es decir que el grupo de palabras tiene un significado completo. A veces un grupo de palabras tiene un sujeto y un verbo pero no llega a expresar un idea completa. Vea los siguientes ejemplos. Los sujetos y verbos han sido marcados para que sean fáciles de ser identificados.

Oraciones completas (también llamadas clausulas independientes):

I left an hour earlier than usual.

Our **team finished** its year-end evaluation.

Roger tried to explain his position.

Oraciones fragmentadas o incompletas (clausulas dependientes):

If **I left** an hour earlier than usual.

When our **team finished** its year-end evaluation.

Whenever **Roger tried** to explain his position.

La proxima sección explica por qué grupos de palabras en el segundo grupo no son oraciones completas.

ORACIONES FRAGMENTADAS

En el ejemplo anterior, usted se habrá dado cuenta de que cada fragmento es más largo que la misma oración completa. Por otro lado, el grupo de palabras sigue siendo el mismo, pero los fragmentos tienen una palabra extra al comienzo. Estas palabras son conocidas como *conjunciones subordinadas.* Si un grupo de palabras que normalmente constituiría una oración completa es precedida por una conjunción subordinada, se necesita algo más para completar la oración. Estas oraciones o cláusulas dependientes, necesitan de algo más para completar su significado; por lo tanto, ellas *dependen* de una *cláusula independiente,* un grupo de palabras que por sí mismas pueden formar una oración completa. Examine como los fragmentos anteriores fueron escritos para expresar un pensamiento completo.

If I left an hour earlier than usual, I would be able to avoid rush hour.

When our team finished its year-end evaluation, we all took the next day off.

Whenever Roger tried to explain his position, he misquoted the facts.

Estas palabras pueden ser usadas como conjunciones subordinadas:

after	once	until
although	since	when
as	than	whenever
because	that	where
before	though	wherever
if	unless	while

A veces una conjunción subordinada es una frase en lugar de una sóla palabra:

as if we didn't already know

as though she had always lived in the town

as long as they can still be heard

as soon as I can finish my work

even though you aren't quite ready

in order that we may proceed more carefully

so that all of us understand exactly

Cláusulas subordinadas usadas como oraciones son sólo un tipo de oración fragmentada. Vea los ejemplos que siguen. Para cada pregunta, elija el grupo de palabras que forma una oración completa y ponga la letra correspondiente en el espacio indicado a la derecha. Vea si usted se puede darse cuenta de la similaridades entre grupos de palabras y fragmentos.

Grupo de palabras A	Grupo de palabras B	?
1. We are ready for the next task.	Washing the car.	☐
2. Seeing the plane arriving.	Heather's family rushed to the gate.	☐
3. Broken down after years of use.	The receptionist finally got a new phone.	☐
4. We saw Andrea sitting all by herself.	Imagining what Florida was like in March.	☐

Las oraciones completas son 1. A. 2. B, 3. B, y 4. A. Los fragmentos son frases simples. Ellos no tienen sujeto o verbo. Si usted combina los dos tipos de palabras, ambas serán parte de una oración completa. Vea cómo se ha hecho en el ejemplo que sigue. Con algunas de las palabras, todo lo que se necesita es una coma. Con otras, unas cuantas palabras extras tienen que ser añadidas para incorporar la frase en el resto de la oración.

1. We are ready for the next task, which is washing the car.

2. Seeing the plane arriving, Heather's family rushed to the gate.

3. Since the phone was broken down after years of use, the receptionist finally got a new one.

4. We saw Andrea sitting all by herself, imagining what Florida was like in March.

Ahora vea la tabla que sigue. En cada grupo, una de las opciones es una oración completa. La otra es un fragmento. Ponga la letra de la oración completa en el espacio indicado a la derecha. Vea si puede observar algunas similitudes entre los fragmentos.

Grupo de palabras A	Grupo de palabras B	?
1. About the way he combs his hair.	I've noticed something very strange.	☐
2. My aunt is a respiratory therapist.	A person who helps people rebuild their lungs and circulatory system.	☐
3. Benjamin saw a piece of key lime pie.	His favorite type of dessert.	☐
4. And tried to sell popcorn and candy.	We went door to door.	☐
5. During the rest of the afternoon.	Everything went smoothly.	☐
6. Icy roads and hazardous weather.	We couldn't make the deadline.	☐
7. In the parking ramp near our building.	I was fortunate to find a parking spot.	☐
8. And saw the picture of our company's new owner.	We read the morning paper.	☐
9. We traveled through the desert all night.	Without seeing a single car or building.	☐
10. We walked all over downtown.	And applied for part-time jobs at theaters.	☐

Las oraciones completas son 1. B, 2. A, 3. A, 4. B, 5. B, 6. B, 7. B, 8. B, 9. A, and 10.A.

La mayor parte de los fragmentos son frases que pueden ser fácilmente incorporadas dentro de una oración completa usando la cláusula independiente con la cual han sido apareadas. Trate de hacerlo por usted mismo. Compare sus oraciones con las versiones que siguen.

Vea las oraciones 1, 5, 7, y 9. Los fragmentos en estas oraciones no son más que frases separadas de las cláusulas independientes. Lo único que usted necesita hacer es añadir el fragmento a la oración completa en un lugar donde pueda entrar. No son necesarios la puntuación o palabras adicionales.

1. I've noticed something very strange about the way he combs his hair.

5. Everything went smoothly during the rest of the afternoon.

7. I was fortunate to find a spot in the parking ramp near our building.

9. We traveled through the desert all night without seeing a single car or building.

Ahora examine las oraciones 2 y 3. Estos fragmentos son frases que explican o identifican detalladamente algo de la oración completa. Dichas frases son llamadas frases *appositivas*. Lo único que necesita hacer es poner una coma después de la palabra que se explica o se identifica, y luego añadir la frase appositiva.

2. My aunt is a respiratory therapist, a person who helps people rebuild their lungs and respiratory system.

3. Benjamin saw key lime pie, his favorite type of dessert.

Observe las oraciones 4, 8, y 10. En estas oraciones, el fragmento es un verbo (acción) separado de la cláusula independiente o de la oración completa. Lo que se necesita es añadir el fragmento a la oración.

4. We went door to door and tried to sell popcorn and candy.

8. We read the morning paper and saw the picture of our company's new owner.

10. We walked all over downtown and applied for part-time jobs at theaters.

Finalmente, vea la oración 6. En esta oración, las palabras extras son necesarias para añadir el fragmento a la oración.

6. We couldn't make the deadline because of the icy roads and hazardous weather.

ORACIONES SIN PUNTUACIÓN

Una cláusula *independiente* es un grupo de palabras que puede ser por sí misma una oración completa. Una oración sin puntuación (punto final, punto y coma, coma).

Ejemplos:

Lynn moved from Minneapolis her job was transferred.

The concert seemed unending it lasted almost until midnight.

We got some gas then we headed off to Omaha.

Todos los tres ejemplos pueden ser corregidos fácilmente de una de las tres maneras:

- Al añadir un punto final y una mayúscula.

  Lynn moved from Minneapolis. Her job was transferred.

  The concert seemed unending. It lasted almost until midnight.

  We got some gas. Then we headed off to Omaha.

- Al añadir una coma y una conjunción (*and, but, or, for, not, yet, so*) muchas veces uno tiene que cambiar el orden de las palabras.

  Lynn's job was transferred, and she moved from Minneapolis.

  The concert seemed unending, for it lasted almost until midnight.

  We got some gas, and then we headed off to Omaha.

■ Convirtiendo una de las cláusulas independientes en una cláusula dependiente. Para hacer esto se necesita añadir una conjunción subordinada que pueda entrar en la oración. Esto generalmente se puede hacer de muchas maneras cambiando nombres a las cláusulas o usando diferentes tipos de conjunciones subordinadas. ¿Recuerde la lista de conjunciones subordinadas que usted vió al principio de este libro?

Lynn moved from Minneapolis because her job was transferred.

When her job was transferred, Lynn moved from Minneapolis.

Since the concert lasted almost until midnight, it seemed unending.

The concert seemed unending because it lasted until almost midnight.

After we got some gas, we headed off to Omaha.

We headed off to Omaha after we got some gas.

PRÁCTICA

Elija las respuestas que incluyan *sólo* oraciones privadas. Tenga cuidado con los fragmentos y con las oraciones sin puntuación. Las respuestas están al final de este libro.

1. a. The huge northern pike snapped my line. And took my favorite lure.
   b. The huge northern pike snapped my line and took my favorite lure.

2. a. Cathy is a good organizer. She chairs the newly formed committee.
   b. Cathy is a good organizer she chairs the newly formed committee.

3. a. The lights were on in the house we assumed you were at home.
   b. The lights were on in the house. We assumed you were at home.

4. a. Andy showed a great deal of promise. After only his first month of work.
   b. Andy showed a great deal of promise after only his first month of work.

5. a. You will find the manual inside the right-hand drawer of my desk.
   b. You will find the manual. Inside the right-hand drawer of my desk.

6. a. Sally needs additional time to complete the project it is more complicated than we thought.
   b. Sally needs additional time to complete the project. It is more complicated than we thought.

7. a. After Mavis wrote the program, Sam edited it.
   b. Mavis wrote the program Sam edited it.

8. a. Bob signed the application he gave it to the interviewer.
   b. Bob signed the application, and he gave it to the interviewer.

9. a. Edsel was ready for the auditor his department's books were all in order.

    b. Edsel was ready for the auditor since his department's books were all in order.

10. a. Alexis found a part-time job that supplemented her income.

    b. Alexis found a part-time job. Supplemented her income.

ORACIONES CON USOS INCORRECTOS DE COMAS

Una oración con el uso incorrecto de comas es la última clase de oraciones incorrectas que va a estudiar hoy. Este tipo de oración es un caso especial de oración sin puntuación ya que en ésta la coma es usada en lugar de un punto y coma para unir, sin una conjunción, dos cláusulas independientes. Este uso incorrecto de la coma puede ser corregido al introducir un punto y coma en lugar de la coma o al añadir una conjunción después de la coma.

Incorrecto

    Henry lives across the street, he has been there for 25 years.

Correcto

    Henry lives across the street; he has been there for 25 years.

    Henry lives across the street, and he has been there for 25 years.

Incorrecto

    Mary heads the search committee, John is the recorder.

Correcto

    Mary heads the search committee; John is the recorder.

    Mary heads the search committee, and John is the recorder.

Incorrecto

    Sid gave demonstrations all summer long, he returned in the fall.

Correcto

    Sid gave demonstrations all summer long; he returned in the fall.

    Sid gave demonstrations all summer long, but he returned in the fall.

PRÁCTICA

Aquí una oportunidad de aplicar lo que usted ha aprendido acerca de las oraciones incompletas, los fragmentos, las oraciones sin puntuación, y el uso incorrecto de la coma. En cada uno de los grupos de palabras que siguen decida si éste constituye una oración escrita correctamente (O), si es un fragamento (F), una oración sin puntuación (OSP), o una en que se usa incorrectamente la coma (OIC). Use estas abreviaciones, anótelas al lado de cada número, revise su trabajo y compárelo con la página de repuestas al final de la lección. Quizás llegue a reconocer algunas de estas oraciones que son del ejemplo del párrafo inicial. Ahora usted sabe cómo corregir las oraciones que no constituyen oraciones completas.

11. Dr. Anders left detailed care instructions for the patient. A personal friend of his.

12. The night before someone from Publisher's Clearinghouse had called. To tell me that I would be receiving a prize package worth potentially millions of dollars.

13. I was so excited because unlike the other offers, this really sounded legitimate, it sounded to me as though I might really win something this time.

14. I hastily opened the mailbox. Hoping to find the promised envelope.

15. There it was. The promised letter.

16. When I finally finished reading the entire mailing.

17. The officer responded to the call, he received it at 8:10 P.M.

18. Emily posted the last transaction it was time to close the books for the day.

19. Our new computer system is still not working properly.

20. Hanging over the doorway in the office next to the conference room.

Escribe de nuevo los fragmentos, oraciones sin puntuación, usos incorrectos de comas como oraciones completas.

Técnicas de aprendizaje

Lea el párrafo al comienzo de la lección, revíselo par eliminar la fragmentación de la oración, el uso incorrecto de comas, y la mala puntuación. A medida que lee el periódico matinal o algún material escrito en el trabajo, busque oraciones que pueden ser incorrectas. Si no encuentra error alguno, busque las oraciones completas que puedan ser combinadas. Las oportunidades son muchas especialmente en los periódicos. Usted también podrá encontrar errores, especialmente fragmentos, en los anuncions publicitarios. Practique escribiendo oraciones completas en cualquier trabajo escrito que se le asigne.

Respuestas

1. b.	**6.** b.	**11.** F	**16.** F
2. a.	**7.** a.	**12.** F	**17.** OIC
3. b.	**8.** b.	**13.** OIC	**18.** OSP
4. b.	**9.** b.	**14.** F	**19.** O
5. a.	**10.** a.	**15.** F	**20.** F

4

USO DE COMAS Y LAS PARTES DE UNA ORACIÓN

RESUMEN DE LA LECCIÓN

Esta y la próxima lección se tratan del uso de comas. La lección de hoy se trata de la relación de las comas con las diferentes partes de una oración, como en las cláusulas y las frases.

Durante el estudio de esta lección usted aprenderá como usar comas en relación con las partes de una oración. A medida que usted avance la lección, recuerde lo que ha aprendido sobre las oraciones y sus errores en la lección anterior. Antes de empezar, vea cuanto ya sabe sobre comas y partes de una oración. Añada comas donde cree que deben de estar en la versión de **PROBLEMA** que aparece en la siguiente página. Evalúese a sí mismo comparando sus respuestas con la versión de la **SOLUCIÓN** en la sección que sigue.

Problema	Solución
Startled I looked up to see a bird flying around the office.	Startled, I looked up to see a bird flying around the office.
After examining the report carefully Edith printed a final copy and mailed it.	After examining the report carefully, Edith printed a final copy and mailed it.
As soon as we finish this last round we can quit for the day.	As soon as we finish this last round, we can quit for the day.
Thinking carefully about the needs of the customers Randall revised his sales plan.	Thinking carefully about the needs of the customers, Randall revised his sales plan.
Because production falls during the winter months we will cut one daily shift.	Because production falls during the winter months, we will cut one daily shift.
Like a confused duckling Richard waddled through the mound of paperwork.	Like a confused duckling, Richard waddled through the mound of paperwork.
She spends a great deal of time listening to the problems of her customers who have come to depend on her advice.	She spends a great deal of time listening to the problems of her customers, who have come to depend on her advice.
Zig Ziglar the last motivational speaker brought the convention crowd to their feet.	Zig Ziglar, the last motivational speaker, brought the convention crowd to their feet.
The cable car which I am waiting for is already twenty minutes late.	The cable car, which I am waiting for, is already twenty minutes late.

USO DE COMAS DESPUÉS DE PALABRAS DE INTRODUCCIÓN, FRASES Y CLÁUSULAS

Use una coma para establecer el uso de palabras de introducción, de frases y cláusulas contenidas en la parte principal de una oración. La coma previene que el lector automáticamente adhiera la porción introductoría a la parte principal de una oración, y que accidentalmente vuelva a leer la misma oración. En otras palabras, comas que siguen los elementos de introducción ahorran tiempo para el lector y reducen las posibilidades de que éste mal interprete lo que usted ha escrito. Examine los ejemplos que siguen para ver cómo palabras de introducción, frases, y cláusulas son establecidas por las comas.

Palabras:

Disappointed, we left the movie before it ended.

Annoyed, the manager stomped back into the storeroom.

Amazed, Captain Holland dismissed the rest of the troops.

Frases:

Expecting the worst, we liquidated most of our inventory.

Badly injured in the accident, the president was gone for two months.

Reluctant to make matters any worse, the doctor called in a specialist.

Cláusulas:

If we plan carefully for the grand opening, we can increase sales.

While we were eating lunch, an important fax came.

Because we left before the meeting ended, we were not eligible to win a door prize.

¿Recuerda la sección sobre fragmentos de la Lección 3? Una parte de ella se relacionaba con cláusulas subordinadas o dependientes. En los últimos ejemplos de la sección anterior usted pudo observar cláusulas subordinadas o dependientes. La primera parte de cada oración, la cláusula subordinada o dependiente, es seguida por una coma. Las otras dos partes de cada oración podrían ser fácilmente revertidas y la oración todavía tendría sentido. De todas maneras, si usted revierte las partes de la oración, y hace que la cláusula independiente sea la primera cláusula de la oración, usted **NO** necesitará una coma.

Cláusulas subordinadas (*después*) de la cláusula independiente:

We can increase sales if we plan carefully for the grand opening.

An important fax came while we were eating lunch.

We were not eligible to win a door prize because we left before the meeting ended.

PRÁCTICA

Elija de entre los siguentes grupos, la oración correctamente escrita. Las respuestas son provistas al final de la lección.

1. a. Content for the first time in his life, Bryce returned to school.

    b. Content for the first time in his life Bryce returned to school.

2. a. As far as I'm concerned we can call this project a success.

    b. As far as I'm concerned, we can call this project a success.

3. a. I will never forget this moment, as long as I live.

    b. I will never forget this moment as long as I live.

4. a. By the time we finally made up our minds, the contract had been awarded to someone else.

    b. By the time we finally made up our minds the contract had been awarded to someone else.

5. a. Indignant, Mr. Caster left the restaurant without leaving a tip.

    b. Indignant Mr. Caster left the restaurant without leaving a tip.

6. a. Wayne was delighted when he found out he'd been awarded the leading role in the show.

b. Wayne was delighted, when he found out he'd been awarded the leading role in the show.

7. a. By designing the program ourselves, we saved a great deal of expense.

b. By designing the program ourselves we saved a great deal of expense.

8. a. I began working for this company, before I was sixteen.

b. Before I was sixteen, I began working for this company.

9. a. Dripping with water from head to toe, Angie climbed the bank of the river.

b. Dripping with water from head to toe Angie climbed the bank of the river.

10. a. The company honored its oldest employee at the annual meeting.

b. The company honored its oldest employee, at the annual meeting.

Las comas ayudan al lector a reconocer que palabras estan juntas o relacionadas. Añada comas en las siguientes oraciones para que su significado sea más claro.

1. Inside the house was clean and tastefully decorated.

2. After running the greyhounds settled back into their boxes.

3. Alone at night time seems endless.

4. As he watched the game slowly came to an end.

You should have marked the sentences like this:

1. Inside, the house was clean and tastefully decorated.

2. After running, the greyhounds settled back into their boxes.

3. Alone at night, time seems endless.

4. As he watched, the game slowly came to an end.

COMAS CON APOSITIVOS

Un *apositivo* es una palabra o un grupo de palabras que siguen inmediatamente un nombre o pronombre. El apositivo hace que el nombre o el pronombre sea más claro o más definido al explicarlo o identificarlo. Vea estos ejemplos. Los apositivos y frases apositivas han sido marcados.

Ejemplos:

Rachel Stein won the first prize, **an expense-paid vacation to the Bahamas.**

New Orleans, **home of the Saints**, is one of my favorite cities.

One of the most inspiring motivators in college basketball is Dr. Tom Davis, **coach of the Iowa Hawkeyes.**

Algunas veces un nombre propio que identifica o explica en detalle sigue un nombre o pronombre. A pesar de que éste es también un tipo de apositivo, no lleva comas.

Ejemplos:

My sister **Deb** lives four hours away.

The noted novelist **Barbara Kingsolver** writes about the South and Southwest.

The president **Manuel Diaz** will visit this site tomorrow.

En las siguientes oraciones, ponga comas donde sean necesarias.

1. *Megabyte*, a word virtually unheard of a decade ago is very common today.

2. Mrs. McCord the investment specialist left a message for you this afternoon.

3. Jane likes to spend Saturday mornings at the local farmer's market a feast for the senses.

4. Water purity a major concern for campers has steadily worsened over the years.

5. High heels were invented by Louis XIV a very short French king.

6. My aunt Marsha will visit later this month.

Debe haber puntudo la oración de tal manera:

1. *Megabyte*, a word virtually unheard of a decade ago, is very common today.

2. Mrs. McCord, the investment specialist, left a message for you this afternoon.

3. Jane likes to spend Saturday mornings at the local farmer's market, a feast for the senses.

4. Water purity, a major concern for campers, has steadily worsened over the years.

5. High heels were invented by Louis XIV, a very short French king.

6. My aunt Marsha will visit later this month. (no comma needed)

COMAS Y CLÁUSULAS NO-RESTRICTIVAS

Anteriormente en esta lección usted aprendió que una cláusula subordinada al principio de una oración es seguida por una coma, pero la misma, en otra parte dentro de la oración, no es introducida por una coma. Esto es verdad sólo si la cláusula es una cláusula esencial. En algunas oraciones una cláusula no puede ser omitida sin que las oraciones cambien su significado básico. Omitir dicha cláusula hace que el significado o la validez de la oración cambie. Dicha cláusula es conocida como una cláusula *esencial* o *restrictiva*.

Ejemplo:

All drivers **who have had a drunk driving conviction** should have their licenses revoked.

All drivers should have their licenses revoked.

La cláusula marcada es esencial porque el significado de la oración cambia drásticamente si se omite la cláusula de la oración. Una cláusula restrictiva no es establecida por comas.

De todas maneras, una cláusula *no-restrictiva* o *no-esencial* necesita ser establecida por comas. Una cláusula es no-restrictiva si simplemente añade información que no es esencial en el sentido básico de la oración. Si una cláusula no-restrictiva es omitida, el sentido básico de la oración no cambia.

Ejemplo:

My father, **who is still farming,** is 74 years old.

My father is 74 years old.

La cláusula no-restrictiva ha sido marcada. Si se la quita de la oración, el significado básico de la misma no cambia. Cláusula no-restrictivas generalmente comienzan con una de las conjunciones subordinadas: *who, whom, whose, which,* o *that.* (Técnicamente, la conjunción subordinada propia para una cláusula restrictiva es *that*, mientras que cláusulas no-restrictivas usan *which*. En la práctica, muchos autores ignoran esta diferencia.)

PRÁCTICA

Cada una de las oraciones en la tabla que sigue contiene una cláusula subordinada. Éstas han sido marcadas para usted. Si la cláusula es restrictiva o esencial, escriba **R** en el cuadrado de la derecha. Si la cláusula es no-restrictiva, o no-esencial, ponga una **N** en el cuadrado y ponga comas al comenzio de la cláusula. Las respuestas están al final de la lección.

11. Matt **who loves to play video games** is interested in a computer science career. ☐

12. My grandfather **who was born in Berlin** speaks with a German accent. ☐

13. James **who is very shy** had a great deal of trouble with his first speech. ☐

14. The hotel pays the parking ramp fees for anyone **who is a registered guest.** ☐

15. People **who are born on February 29** grow old more slowly than the rest of us. ☐

16. Animals **that have backbones** are called vertebrates. ☐

17. Nicotine **which is present in tobacco products** is a powerful poison.

18. Many Scandinavian names end with sen or son **both of which mean son of.**

19. We live on Fleur Drive **which is right next to the airport.**

20. Mrs. Olson is not a teacher **who takes homework lightly.**

REPASO

El próximo ejercicio es un repaso de todo lo que usted ha aprendido hasta este momento. El párrafo que sigue a continuación no contiene comas, signos de puntuación, o uso de mayúsculas. Use todo lo que hasta ahora ha aprendido. Añada mayúsculas, signos de puntuación, y comas para dar sentido a la versión del párrafo que se encuentra debajo de **Problema.** Revise su trabajo y compárelo con la versión que sigue debajo de la **Solución.**

Problema

even though peter liked his job a great deal he always looked forward to his summer vacation it was the highlight of his year usually he spent two weeks in the middle of july at camp wi wi tq which was forty miles from his home he was responsible for six physically challenged children for 24 hrs a day for two wks how he loved camp

peter took the counseling job one he loved dearly very seriously each morning he rose before the first child awoke and never went to bed until the last of his kids went to sleep at night the best part of the job was challenging the kids to do things for themselves peter would insist that they comb their hair or cut their own food even if they begged for help the camp dean and some of the other counselors thought peter was slacking on the job but he didn't see it that way he enjoyed knowing that his kids left camp more capable and confident than they had been when they arrived

Solución

Even though Peter liked his job a great deal, he always looked forward to his summer vacation. It was the highlight of his year. Usually, he spent two weeks in the middle of July at Camp Wi Wi Ta, which was forty miles from his home. He was responsible for six physically challenged children for 24 hrs. a day for two wks. How he loved camp!

Peter took the counseling job, one he loved dearly, very seriously. Each morning he rose before the first child awoke and never went to bed until the last of his kids went to sleep at night. The best part of the job was challenging the kids to do things for themselves. Peter would insist that they comb their hair or cut their own food even if they begged for help. The camp dean and some of the other counselors thought Peter was slacking on the job, but he didn't see it that way. He enjoyed knowing that his kids left camp more capable and confident than they had been when they arrived.

Técnicas de aprendizaje

Como usted ha podido ver en esta lección, el omitir comas antes de los elementos de introducción o posisionándolas erróneamente al rededor de cláusulas restrictivas, puede ocasionar lecturas un tanto cómicas. Escriba algunas oraciones carentes de comas y que sean un tanto difíciles de leer. Por ejemplo: "As they ate the horse moved closer." Luego corrija sus oraciones añadiendo comas.

RESPUESTAS

1. a.
2. b.
3. b.
4. a.
5. a.
6. a.
7. a.
8. b.
9. a.
10. a.
11. **N** Matt, who loves to play video games, is interested in a computer science career.
12. **N** My grandfather, who was born in Berlin, speaks with a German accent.

13. **N** James, who is very shy, had a great deal of trouble with his first speech.
14. **R** Las comas no son necesarias.
15. **R** Las comas no son necesarias.
16. **R** Las comas no son necesarias.
17. **N** Nicotine, which is present in tobacco products, is a powerful poison.
18. **N** Many Scandinavian names end with *son* or *sen*, both of which mean *son of*.
19. **N** We live on Fleur Drive, which is right next to the airport.
20. **R** Las comas no son necesarias.

L·E·C·C·I·Ó·N 5

COMAS QUE AYUDAN A SEPARAR

RESUMEN DE LA LECCIÓN

Aparte de establecer partes de una oración, comas son usadas en muchas otras situaciones. Esta lección hace un repaso de las ocasiones en las cuales usted debería usar comas para separar elementos dentro de una oración.

Las comas son usadas para separar o clarificar la relación entre las diferentes partes de oraciones para que el significado de las mismas sea claro y fácil de entender. En esta lección usted aprenderá cómo usar comas para separar cláusulas independientes, elementos en una serie, elementos en una fecha o dirección, y palabras que interrumpen el flujo de ideas en una oración. La última parte de la lección explica cómo usar comas en los encabezamientos y despedidas en una carta amistosa.

Comience por determinar cúanto sabe sobre comas que separan. Añada comas donde usted cree que son necesarias en la columna de **Problema** en la página que sigue. Revise su trabajo y compárelo con la versión de la columna **Solución**. Trate de identificar las reglas aplicables a las preguntas que contestó mal a través de la lección.

Problema

Dear Aunt Jan

I hate to give you my whole life story so I'll start halfway through. When I began my first full-time job I was twenty-one years old a freshly scrubbed college graduate. I worked as an English teacher at Sioux Valley Schools 721 Straight Row Drive Linn Grove Iowa. My first day of teacher workshops was August 28 1976 and I came armed with a nice clean notebook a pen a pencil and a new three-ring binder. I expected a day of meetings but I got nothing of the sort. The only time the entire staff got together was at noon when the principal announced that the parents group had set up a lunch for us in the cafeteria. What a feast: fresh sweet corn vine-ripened tomatoes new potatoes and grilled hamburgers. The president of the school board cooked the burgers nothing less than prime Iowa beef to perfection. It was a first day as you might imagine that I will never forget. I'm looking forward to your next letter.

Sincerely

Solución

Dear Aunt Jan,

I hate to give you my whole life story, so I'll start halfway through. When I began my first full-time job, I was twenty-one years old, a freshly scrubbed college graduate. I worked as an English teacher at Sioux Valley Schools, 721 Straight Row Drive, Linn Grove, Iowa. My first day of teacher workshops was August 28, 1976, and I came armed with a nice, clean notebook, a pen, a pencil and a new three-ring binder. I expected a day of meetings, but I got nothing of the sort. The only time the entire staff got together was at noon when the principal announced that the parents' group had set up a lunch for us in the cafeteria. What a feast: fresh sweet corn, vine-ripened tomatoes, new potatoes and grilled hamburgers. The president of the school board cooked the burgers, nothing less than prime Iowa beef, to perfection. It was a first day, as you might imagine, that I will never forget. I'm looking forward to your next letter.

Sincerely,

COMAS CON CLÁUSULAS INDEPENDIENTES UNIDAS POR UNA CONJUNCIÓN

Como usted debe recordar de la Lección 3, una *cláusula independiente* es un grupo de palabras que puede ser independientemente establecida como una oración completa. Una *conjunción* es una palabra unificadora: *and, but, or, for, nor, so,* o *yet.* A veces el escritor combinará dos o más cláusulas independientes para formar una oración compuesta. Si una conjunción une las cláusulas, ponga una coma después de cada cláusula. Las comas y conjunciones son marcadas en los siguientes ejemplos.

Ejemplos:

I went to bed early last night, **so** I felt rested this morning.

The city's economic situation has improved, **but** there are still neighborhoods where many people depend on the generosity of others in order to live.

Susan worked through lunch, **and** now she is able to leave the office early.

Si las cláusulas independientes están unidas *sin* una conjunción, éstas están separadas por un punto y coma en lugar de una coma.

Ejemplos:

I went to bed early last night; I felt rested this morning.

The city's economic situation has improved; however, there are still neighborhoods where many people depend on the generosity of others in order to live.

Susan worked through lunch; now she is able to leave the office early.

PRÁCTICA

Use comas y puntos y comas para puntuar correctamente las siguientes oraciones. Las respuestas se encuentran al final de la lección.

1. You can safely view an eclipse through the viewing glass of a welding helmet or you can look through a piece of overexposed film.

2. The prisoner showed no remorse as the guilty verdict was announced nor did the tears of the victim's family arouse any emotion.

3. The young calf put its head over the fence and it licked my hand and sucked on my fingers.

4. Icebergs in the Antarctic are flat and smooth but those in the Arctic are rough.

5. I understand your position on this issue I still believe you are dead wrong.

6. I like Sam he likes me for we are best of friends.

7. The inventory is valued at one million dollars but it's not enough to cover our debt.

8. If you know of anyone with data processing experience encourage him or her to apply for this new position.

COMAS PARA SEPARAR PARTES EN UNA SERIE

Para facilitar la lectura y el entendimiento de la materia para el lector, las comas son usadas para separar partes de listas de palabras semejantes, frases, o cláusulas. La última parte en una serie suele ser precedida por una conjunción. Hablando con propiedad, no se necesita una coma antes de la conjunción. (De todas maneras, y para evitar cualquier tipo de confusión, muchos escritores—incluso algunos escritores de pruebas—prefieren usar comas antes de la conjunción final.)

Ejemplos:

Al, Jane, Herbert, and Willis all applied for the promotion.

The old Tempo's engine squealed loudly, shook violently, and ground to a halt.

The instructions clearly showed how to assemble the equipment, how to load the software, and how to boot the system.

Si cada parte de la serie está separada por una conjunción, las comas no son necesarias.

Ejemplo:

Billie and Charles and Cameron performed at the company Christmas party.

COMAS PARA SEPARAR PARTES EN UNA FECHA O UNA DIRECCIÓN

Cuando uno da una fecha completa en el formato *month-day-year,* ponga una coma en ambos lados del año. Cuando da una fecha que solamente contiene el mes y el año, la coma no es necesaria.

Use una coma para separar cada elemento de una dirección, como por ejemplo calle, ciudad, estado, y país. También se usa una coma después del estado o el país si es que la oración continua después de la dirección.

Ejemplos:

We moved from Fayetteville, North Carolina, on May 16, 1993.

Since November 1994, Terry has lived at 654 36th Street, Lincoln, Nebraska.

Dwana attended Drake University, Des Moines, Iowa, both fall 1994 and spring 1995.

PRÁCTICA

En las siguientes oraciones añada comas y puntuaciones finales donde sean necesarias. Use no sólo lo que está aprendiendo en esta lección sino también lo que aprendió en la Lección 4. Las respuestas aparecen al final de la lección.

9. After he ran into the mayor's car with his truck Adam used his cellular phone to call the police his doctor his lawyer and his insurance agent.

10. The homegrown philosopher who lives next door at 251 Acorn Street Libertyville Kansas claims to know exactly who invented the wheel sliced bread and kissing.

11. Estelle was born on January 31 1953 and Arun was born on June 30 1960.

12. Looking for a solution to the printing problem Karissa asked an older employee questioned the supervisor and finally consulted the printer manual.

13. Baruch brought a jello salad to the potluck Shannon brought peanuts M & M's mints and pretzels.

COMAS PARA SEPARAR ADJETIVOS

Use comas para separar dos o más adjetivos igualmente importantes.

Ejemplos:
Alex avoided the **friendly, talkative, pleasant** boy sitting next to him at school.
The carpenter repaired the floor with **dark, aged, oak** flooring.
The reporter spoke with several **intense, talented** high school athletes.

Ponga mucha atención a la oración que acaba de leer. Usted se dará cuenta de que las palabras *several, high,* y *school* son también adjetivos que modifican *athletes*. No todos los adjetivos que modifican la misma palabra son igualmente importantes. Sólo aquellos de importancia igual son separados por una coma. Si usted pone en práctica uno o dos de estas pruebas, usted puede facilmente determinar si es que el uso de una coma es necesario:

- Cambie el orden de los adjetivos. Si la oración se lee tan claramente como antes de cambiar el orden de los adjetivos, sepárelos usando comas. Si la oración no está clara o suena mal, no use las comas. Los primeros dos ejemplos anteriores de oraciones tienen sentido incluso si la posición de sus adjetivos no es la misma. El último ejemplo no tiene sentido si usted cambia el orden de los adjetivos *intense* y *talented*. Por consiguiente, esos son los únicos adjetivos separados por comas.
  - ✓ Alex avoided the **talkative, friendly, pleasant** boy sitting next to him at school.
  - ✓ The carpenter repaired the floor with **aged, dark, oak** flooring.
  - ✗ The reporter spoke with **intense, several, high, talented, school** athletes.

- Una segunda e igualmente efectiva prueba es colocar *and* entre medio de los adjetivos. Si la oración se sigue leyendo correctamente, entonces use comas entre los adjetivos. Si la oración suena extraña o incorrecta, no use las comas. Nuevamente, esto funciona con el primer ejemplo de las dos oraciones, pero en la última oración *and* sólo tiene sentido cuando está entre *intense* y *talented*. Trate estas dos pruebas con las siguientes oraciones. ¿Dónde se ponen las comas?
  We bought an **antique wrought iron** daybed.
  The envelope contained **three crisp clean brand new** hundred dollar bills.

Usted debería de haber puntuado las oraciones de la siguiente manera:

> We bought an **antique, wrought iron** daybed.
>
> The envelope contained **three crisp, clean, brand new** hundred dollar bills.

COMAS PARA SEPARAR OTROS ELEMENTOS DE UNA ORACIÓN

- Use comas para separar elementos contrastantes u opuestos en una oración. La coma funciona como una señal para el lector: Lo que sigue es una idea opuesta. Ésta hace que el lector pueda captar la idea más fácilmente.
  Ejemplos:
    We searched the entire house, **but found nothing**.

    We need strong intellects, **not strong bodies,** to resolve this problem.

    The racers ran slowly at first, **quickly at the end**.

    We expected to meet the President, **not a White House aide**.

- Use comas para separar palabras o frases que interrumpen el flujo de ideas en una oración.
  Ejemplos:
    The deadline, **it seemed clear,** simply could not be met.

    We came to rely, **however,** on the kindness and generosity of the neighbors.

    The alternative route, **we discovered,** was faster than the original route.

- Cuando el nombre de una persona a la que uno se dirije está incluida en una oración, ésta debe iniciarse con una coma.
  Ejemplos:
    Dave, we wanted you to look at this layout before we sent it to printing.

    We wanted you to look at this layout, **Dave,** before we sent it to printing.

    We wanted you to look at this layout before we sent it to printing, **Dave**.

- Exclamaciones no muy fuertes incluidas en una oración también deben inicializarce con comas.
  Ejemplos:
    Well, that was certainly a pleasant surprise.

    Yes, I'll call you as soon as we get the information.

    Heavens, that was a long-winded speaker.

- Use una coma después del encabezamiento o la despedida de un carta amistosa.
  Ejemplos:
    Dear Uncle Jon,

    Sincerely yours,

    Yours truly,

PRÁCTICA

Elija la versión con la puntuación correcta de cada uno de los siguientes grupos de oraciones. Esté al tanto de lo que ha aprendido sobre el uso de la coma en la lección anterior.

14. a. No, I haven't received a reply just yet, but I expect one any day.

   b. No I haven't received a reply just yet, but I expect one any day.

   c. No, I haven't received a reply just yet but I expect one any day.

15. a. My steak was burned to a crisp, the burger, on the other hand, was dripping with blood.

   b. My steak was burned to a crisp; the burger, on the other hand, was dripping with blood.

   c. My steak was burned to a crisp, the burger, on the other hand was dripping with blood.

16. a. Well, Sancha, I wonder if Mindy made it to her interview on time.

   b. Well, Sancha I wonder if Mindy made it to her interview on time.

   c. Well Sancha, I wonder if Mindy made it to her interview on time.

17. a. When we go on vacation, we need to remember our clothing fishing equipment and cameras.

   b. When we go on vacation we need to remember our clothing, fishing equipment, and cameras.

   c. When we go on vacation, we need to remember our clothing, fishing equipment, and cameras.

18. a. The correct address I believe is 215 North 34th, Streator, Illinois.

   b. The correct address, I believe, is 215 North 34th, Streator, Illinois.

   c. The correct address, I believe, is 215, North 34th, Streator, Illinois.

19. a. Our newest employee, a transfer from the home office, is the strong silent absent type, I think.

   b. Our newest employee, a transfer from the home office is the strong, silent, absent type, I think.

   c. Our newest employee, a transfer from the home office, is the strong, silent, absent type, I think.

20. a. I'm afraid, Mr. Dobbs, that you lack the qualifications for this job; but we have another that might interest you.

   b. I'm afraid Mr. Dobbs, that you lack the qualifications for this job, but we have another that might interest you.

   c. I'm afraid, Mr. Dobbs, that you lack the qualifications for this job, but we have another that might interest you.

21. a. Usually, at the company picnic we play badminton, frisbee golf, volleyball, and horseshoes.
   b. Usually, at the company picnic, we play badminton frisbee golf, volleyball and horseshoes.
   c. Usually, at the company picnic we play badminton, frisbee, golf, volleyball, and horseshoes.

22. a. We will advertise our biggest sale of the decade on June 21, 1997, the 25th anniversary of our Grand Opening sale.
   b. We will advertise our biggest sale of the decade on June 21 1997, the 25th anniversary of our Grand Opening sale.
   c. We will advertise our biggest sale of the decade on June 21, 1997 the 25th anniversary of our Grand Opening sale.

23. a. Exhausted by the heat, rather than the exertion, Ming collapsed under a tall shady oak tree.
   b. Exhausted by the heat rather than the exertion, Ming collapsed under a tall, shady oak tree.
   c. Exhausted by the heat, rather than the exertion, Ming collapsed under a tall, shady oak tree.

Técnicas de aprendizaje

A medida que usted lea un periódico, un libro o materiales escritos del trabajo, ponga mucha atención a las comas que pueda observar. Trate de recordar por qué una coma puede ser usada en cada una de las situaciones. Ya que la coma es una de las marcas de puntuación más mal usadas, busque lugares donde otros escritores la hayan usado incorrectamente.

RESPUESTAS

1. You can safely view an eclipse through the viewing glass of a welding helmet, or you can look through a piece of overexposed film.
2. The prisoner showed no remorse as the guilty verdict was announced, nor did the tears of the victim's family arouse any emotion.
3. The young calf put its head over the fence, and it licked my hand and sucked on my fingers.
4. Icebergs in the Antarctic are flat and smooth, but those in the Arctic are rough.
5. I understand your position on this issue; I still believe you are dead wrong.
6. I like Sam; he likes me, for we are best of friends.
7. The inventory is valued at one million dollars, but it's not enough to cover our debt.
8. If you know of anyone with data processing experience, encourage him or her to apply for this new position.
9. After he ran into the mayor's car with his truck, Adam used his cellular phone to call the police, his doctor, his lawyer, and his insurance agent.
10. The homegrown philosopher who lives next door at 251 Acorn Street, Libertyville, Kansas, claims to know exactly who invented the wheel, sliced bread, and kissing.
11. Estelle was born on January 31, 1953, and Arun was born on June 30, 1960.
12. Looking for a solution to the printing problem, Karissa asked an older employee, questioned the supervisor, and finally consulted the printer manual.
13. Baruch brought a jello salad to the potluck. Shannon brought peanuts, M & M's, mints, and pretzels.
14. a.
15. b.
16. a.
17. c.
18. b.
19. c.
20. c.
21. c.
22. a.
23. c.

PUNTO Y COMA, Y DOS PUNTOS

6

LESSON SUMMARY

Mucha gente se confunde con el uso del punto y coma (;) y el dos puntos (:), depués del estudio de esta lección usted sabrá exactamente como usarlos.

En la lección 3 usted aprendió a usar el punto y coma para separar cláusulas independientes. En esta lección usted examinará el uso del punto y coma así como el uso de otras marcas de puntuación que ya ha estudiado. Usted aprenderá cómo se usa el punto y coma con adverbios conjuntivos y cuándo separar elementos en una serie con puntos y comas. También aprenderá a usar los dos puntos para comunicarse dentro del mundo de los negocios y de otros lugares.

Empiece por ver cuánto sabe. Añada punto y comas y dos puntos donde cree que son necesarios en la columna **Problema** en el lado izquierdo de la próxima página. Revise sus respuestas y compárelas con aquellas de la columna **Solución** que está al lado derecho de la próxima página.

Problema

Dear Mr. Powell

This letter is a formal complaint regarding service our company received from your representatives at 130 P.M. on January 26, 1996. These are the procedures for which we were billed a complete scotomy, a procedure to rid the machinery of electrostatic material a comprehensive assessment, a procedure for checking all mechanical and electronic parts in the machinery a thorough cleaning, a procedure necessary to keep the machine running efficiently.

This may be what the representative reported to have done however, only the first procedure in the list was finished. Only one of the three items was completed therefore, we should be refunded the amount charged for the other two services.

We are filing this complaint in accordance with your technical manual *McDounah New Age Electronics A Complete Manual.* This information is found in Volume 2, page 27 "Customers dissatisfied with our service for any reason have the right to file a full complaint within 10 (ten) days from the date of service. Such a complaint must be addressed in writing to Mr. Douglas Powell, Service Manager McDounah New Age Electronics Demming,

Solución

Dear Mr. Powell:

This letter is a formal complaint regarding service our company received from your representatives at 1:30 P.M. on January 26, 1996. These are the procedures for which we were billed: a complete scotomy, a procedure to rid the machinery of electrostatic material; a comprehensive assessment, a procedure for checking all mechanical and electronic parts in the machinery; a thorough cleaning, a procedure necessary to keep the machine running efficiently.

This may be what the representative reported to have done; however, only the first procedure in the list was finished. Only one of the three items was completed; therefore, we should be refunded the amount charged for the other two services.

We are filing this complaint in accordance with your technical manual *McDounah New Age Electronics: A Complete Manual.* This information is found in Volume 2, page 27: "Customers dissatisfied with our service for any reason have the right to file a full complaint within 10 (ten) days from the date of service. Such a complaint must be addressed in writing to Mr. Douglas Powell, Service Manager; McDounah New Age Electronics; Demming,

(Continua en la proxima página)

Problema (continuación)

Delaware. Mr. Powell will respond within two days to remedy the alleged problem or to refund the amount in question."

We appreciate your prompt attention to this matter.

Sincerely yours,

Solución (continuación)

Delaware. Mr. Powell will respond within two days to remedy the alleged problem or to refund the amount in question."

We appreciate your prompt attention to this matter.

Sincerely yours,

PUNTO Y COMA

Hay tres casos diferentes en los cuales el punto y coma es usado para separar cláusulas independientes. (Vea la Lección 3 si es que se le ha olvidado lo que es una cláusula independiente.)

- Para separar cláusulas independientes unidas sin una conjunción. Esta regla le puede parecer familiar ya que estaba también incluida en la lección anterior.

  Ejemplos:

  Three doctors began the research project; only one completed it.

  Discard the packaging; save the paperwork for accounting.

  The hour is over; it's time to stop working.

- Para separar cláusulas independientes que contienen comas incluso si las cláusulas están unidas con una conjunción. El punto y coma ayuda que el lector vea que se lleva a cabo una interrupción en la idea.

  Ejemplo:

  The team needed new equipment, updated training manuals, and better professional advice; but since none of this was provided, they performed as poorly as they had in the previous competition.

- Para separar cláusulas independientes conectadas por un adverbio conjuntivo. Siga al adverbio con una coma. Un *adverbio conjuntivo* es un adverbio que unifica cláusulas independientes. Adverbios conjuntivos usan una puntuación diferente de las conjunciones regulares. La primera cláusula independiente es seguida por un punto y coma; el adverbio conjuntivo es seguido por una coma.

  Ejemplos:

  Our copy of the central warehouse catalog arrived after the budget deadline; **consequently,** our requests are late.

  In the book *An American Childhood*, Annie Dillard recounts her experiences as a child; **furthermore,** she questions and speculates about the meaning of life.

He aquí una lista completa de palabras usadas como adverbios conjuntivos.

accordingly	furthermore	instead	otherwise
besides	hence	moreover	therefore
consequently	however	nevertheless	thus

Mucha gente confunde las conjunciones subordinadas, como por ejemplo *because, until,* y *while,* con los adverbios conjuntivos anotados anteriormente. La diferencia es importante. Una cláusula que comienza con un conjunción subordinada es sólo una cláusula subordinada; no puede quedar por sí misma como una oración. Una cláusula con un adverbio conjuntivo es una *cláusula independiente,* que tiene que ser separada de otra cláusula de la misma clase por un punto aparte, una mayúscula , o por un punto y coma.

Este es un pequeño truco que le ayudará a determinar si es que una palabra que comienza con una cláusula es un adverbio conjuntivo. Si usted puede mover la palabra a cualquier lugar dentro la cláusula, es un adverbio conjuntivo. Si no puede hacerlo, probablemente es una conjunción subordinada. Éstas son las cláusulas principales:

My paycheck was delayed. I couldn't pay my rent on time.

Éste es un ejemplo de las dos maneras de unir esas dos cláusulas principales:

My paycheck was delayed; therefore, I couldn't pay my rent on time.
I couldn't pay my rent on time because my paycheck was delayed.

Revise si la primera versión incluye el uso de un adverbio conjuntivo. ¿Puede mover *therefore* dentro de la cláusula? Usted puede decir que Sí, "*I couldn't, therefore, pay my rent on time.*" Entonces, *therefore* es un adverbio conjuntivo.

Use el mismo método para evualuar si *because* es un adverbio conjuntivo que debe seguir un punto y coma. ¿Puede usted mover *because* dentro de la cláusula? "My paycheck because was delayed"? No, no se puede porque *because* es una conjunción subordinada, y la cláusula que la está introduciendo no es la clásula principal.

There's one more way a semicolon is used to separate:

- Use el punto y coma para separar elementos en una serie si es que estos elememtos contienen comas. A diferencia de cosas en una serie que pueden ser separados por comas, un punto y coma es usado inclusive cuando HAY una conjunción.

Ejemplos:

The dates we are considering for our annual party are Thursday, **June 5; Saturday, June 7; Sunday, June 8; or** Monday, June 9.

When we go to the lake, I am sure to take a pizza pan, a popcorn popper, and pancake **griddle; fishing** tackle, life jackets, and ski **equipment; and** puzzles, cards, board games, and my guitar.

The expansion committee is considering locations in Columbus, **Ohio; Orange, California; Minton, Tennessee; and** Jacksonville, Florida.

PRÁCTICA

Practique lo que acaba de aprender y añada en la siguientes oraciones los puntos y comas donde sean necesarios. Usted encontrará las respuestas al final de la lección.

1. I need a break I've been working for five hours straight.

2. We have branch offices in Paris, France Berlin, Germany Stockholm, Sweden and Budapest, Hungary.

3. We had no problem meeting the deadline however, we were still able to find ways of streamlining production.

4. We ate swiss steak, riced potatoes, steamed broccoli and fresh bread for dinner but we still had room to eat apple pie for dessert.

5. Paige left some of the confidential documents sitting on her desk at work consequently, she worried about their safety all night long.

DOS PUNTOS

DOS PUNTOS COMO INTRODUCCIÓN

- Use dos puntos para introducir una lista de cosas, siempre y cuando la parte antes de los dos puntos sea una oración completa.

  Ejemplos:

  These people were cast in the play: Andrea, Horatio, Thom, Alley and Benito.

  We packed these items for the trip: cameras, dress clothes, scuba equipment, and beach wear.

- No use dos puntos si la lista de cosas complementa un verbo, en otras palabras, si completa el significado comenzado por el verbo. Vea como ejemplos las oraciones citadas anteriormente y re-escritas de tal manera que el uso de los dos puntos no es necesario.

  Ejemplos:

  The people cast in the play were Kristin, Horatio, Thom, Alley, and Benito.

  For our trip we packed cameras, dress clothes, scuba equipment, and beach wear.

- Use dos puntos para introducir una cita formal.

  Ejemplo:

  John F. Kennedy ended the speech with these notable words: "Ask not what your country can do for you. Ask what you can do for your country."

- Use dos puntos para enfatizar una palabra, frase, o cláusula que añade un énfasis particular a la parte principal de una oración. Nuevamente, la parte antes de los dos puntos tiene que ser una oración completa.

  Ejemplo:

  The financial problems our company has been experiencing have been caused by one thing: poor planning.

  We were missing a vital piece of information: how the basic product design differed from last year's model.

DOS PUNTOS QUE MUESTRAN UNA RELACIÓN SUBORDINADA

Use dos puntos para demostrar una relación subordinada en los siguientes casos:

- Entre dos oraciones cuando la segunda explica la primera.

  Ejemplos:

  Brenton shouted and threw his fists in the air: He had just set a new world's record.

  Nicole put the check into her scrapbook rather than cashing it: It was the first check she had ever earned.

  Scott ignored the phone: He knew it was a salesman for whom he had no time.

- Entre el título y el subtítulo de un libro.

  Ejemplos:

  Internet Starter Kit: A Complete Guide to Cyberspace

  Beyond 2000: A Futuristic View of Time

  O Death, Where is Thy Sting: Tales from the Other Side

- Entre el volumen y el número de página o entre capítulos y versos.

  Ejemplos:

  World Book Encyclopedia V: 128

  New Age Journal of Medicine IX: 23

  John 3:16

  Genesis 1:1

  Psalms 23:2

- Entre la hora y los minutos.

  Ejemplos:

  12:53 A.M.

  2:10 P.M.

- Después del encabezamiento de una carta. Usted aprendió que las comas son usadas después del encabezamiento en cartas personales o amistosas. Dos puntos indica al lector que lo que sigue en la carta es un asunto de negocios o algo que tiene que tomarse en serio. Esto es particularmente cierto si incluye el título pero no el nombre de la persona a quien se dirige la carta. De todas manera, incluso en una carta de negocios, la despedida tiene que ser seguida por una coma.

  Ejemplos:

  Dear Mr. Strange:

  Cordially yours,

Dear Operations Manager:

Respectfully submitted,

PRÁCTICA

Elija la versión con la puntuación correcta de cada uno de los siguientes grupos de oraciones. Puede encontrar las respuestas correctas al final de la lección.

6. a. I found an outline of the procedure in the policy manual, Volume 3: 17.

b. I found an outline of the procedure, in the policy manual, Volume 3: 17.

c. I found an outline of the procedure in the policy manual Volume 3, 17.

7. a. The tornado destroyed most of the buildings on our farm, however the house was untouched by the violent storm.

b. The tornado destroyed most of the buildings on our farm; however the house was untouched by the violent storm.

c. The tornado destroyed most of the buildings on our farm; however, the house was untouched by the violent storm.

8. a. After a week in the woods I need: a towel, a washcloth, a toothbrush, and a bar of soap.

b. After a week in the woods I need a towel, a washcloth, a toothbrush, and a bar of soap.

c. After a week in the woods I need; a towel, a washcloth, a toothbrush, and a bar of soap.

9. a. Dear Subscriber,

Please renew your subscription by 12,00 A.M. on January 5, 1996, to receive the special bonus.

b. Dear Subscriber:

Please renew your subscription by 12:00 A.M. on January 5, 1996, to receive the special bonus.

c. Dear Subscriber;

Please renew your subscription by 12:00 A.M. on January 5, 1996 to receive the special bonus.

10. a. Each day a new shift begins at 8:00 A.M., 4:00 P.M., and 12:00 A.M.

b. Each day a new shift begins at 8:00 A.M.; 4:00 P.M., and 12:00 A.M.

c. Each day a new shift begins at 8:00, A.M.; 4:00, P.M.; and 12:00, A.M.

11. a. I like to play football, a physically challenging sport; chess, a game of logic and strategy; Super Mario World, a mindless Super Nintendo game; and the guitar, a relaxing instrument.

b. I like to play football, a physically challenging sport: chess, a game of logic and strategy: Super Mario World, a mindless Super Nintendo game: and the guitar, a relaxing instrument.

c. I like to play football a physically challenging sport, chess a game of logic and strategy, Super Mario World a mindless Super Nintendo game, and the guitar a relaxing instrument.

12. a. They learned the following information from the interrogation: the suspect's name; the suspect's home address; the suspect's phone number; and the suspect's current employer.

b. They learned the following information from the interrogation the suspect's name, the suspect's home address, the suspect's phone number, and the suspect's current employer.

c. They learned the following information from the interrogation: the suspect's name, the suspect's home address, the suspect's phone number, and the suspect's current employer.

Técnicas de aprendizaje

Vea algunas de las cartas o mensajes que usted ha recibido o escrito últimamente. Examine su puntuación. ¿Usa el autor la forma correcta de marcas de puntuación, de las comas, puntos y comas, puntos aparte? Si no, corríjalos. Será una buena práctica.

RESPUESTAS

1. I need a break; I've been working for five hours straight.
2. We have branch offices in Paris, France; Berlin, Germany; Stockholm, Sweden; and Budapest, Hungary.
3. We had no problem meeting the deadline; however, we were still able to find ways of streamlining production.
4. We ate swiss steak, riced potatoes, steamed broccoli and fresh bread for dinner; but we still had room to eat apple pie for dessert.

5. Paige left some of the confidential documents sitting on her desk at work; consequently, she worried about their safety all night long.
6. a.
7. c.
8. b.
9. b.
10. a.
11. a.
12. c.

7

APÓSTROFES
Y GUIONES

RESUMEN DE LA LECCIÓN

Esta lección le pondrá en control de los apóstrofes (') y los guiones (—), dos de las marcas de puntuación más incorrectamente usadas.

Las apóstrofes comunican información importante del lenguaje escrito. Los guiones, cuando son usados cuidadosamente, añaden énfasis. Antes de comenzar con la lección, vea cuanto usted ya sabe. Añada apóstrofes—y un par de guiones—donde usted cree que deben de estar en la oraciones de la columna **Problema**. Revise por sí mismo y compare sus respuestas con aquellas de la columna **Solución**.

Problema

My grandfather is quite fond of telling stories from the late 30s and early 40s. The Great Depressions effect was beginning to diminish in the small South Dakota town where he lived. He inherited a 160-acre farm after his father-in-laws death in 1938. Little of the farms cropland had produced anything in the years prior to 38. During his first two years as a landowner, he netted a small profit. With the droughts end in 40 came the beginning of good crops. Even with the governments market quotas, he was able to make enough money to buy another quarter of land. He counted on his sons help to farm the addl land, but they went off to Europe when World War II broke out. He purchased a steam engine tractor one of John Deeres first and farmed the 320 acres by himself. That was the beginning of his most successful years as a farmer.

Solución

My grandfather is quite fond of telling stories from the late '30s and early '40s. The Great Depression's effect was beginning to diminish in the small South Dakota town where he lived. He inherited a 160-acre farm after his father-in-law's death in 1938. Little of the farm's cropland had produced anything in the years prior to '38. During his first two years as a landowner, he netted a small profit. With the drought's end in '40 came the beginning of good crops. Even with the government's market quotas, he was able to make enough money to buy another quarter of land. He counted on his sons' help to farm the add'l land, but they went off to Europe when World War II broke out. He purchased a steam engine tractor—one of John Deere's first—and farmed the 320 acres by himself. That was the beginning of his most successful years as a farmer.

APÓSTROFES

PARA DEMOSTRAR PERTENENCIA

Use una apóstrofe para mostrar pertenencia. Las palabras marcadas en cada uno de los ejemplos son *adjetivos posesivos:* Éstas muestran a quién o a qué pertenece el nombre.

Nombres singulares (añada 's)	Nombres plurales que terminan en s (añada ')	Nombre plurales que no terminan en s
boy's toy (The toy is the **boy's**.)	**boys'** bicycles (The bicycles are the **boys'**.)	**men's** schedules (The schedules are the **men's**.)
child's play	**kids'** bedrooms	**children's** opinions
lady's coat	**ladies'** skirts	**women's** department
dentist's aide	**players'** representative	**people's** choice

Las apóstrofes no son usadas para formar plurales. Cuando usted está pensando poner un apóstrofe en un nombre que termina en *s*, pregúntese si usted simplemente está mostrando más de una cosa. Si es así, no hay necesidad de usar un apóstrofe.

Ejemplos:
There are a lot of **potatoes** in the refrigerator.
Cut out the **potatoes'** eyes.

Puede evitar el poner apóstrofes en palabras que son simplemente plurales tratando de esta fórmula: *the _____ of the _____*, como en *the eyes of the potatoes*. Si las palabras no encajan en la fórmula, el nombre no tiene que llevar apóstrofe.

Estos son algunos de los casos especiales para el uso de apóstrofes que demuestran posesión.

- Cuando hay más de una palabra en el adjetivo posesivo—por ejemplo, con un nombre compuesto, un negocio o institución, o cosas pertenecientes a un grupo—añada a la última palabra del nombre compuesto la apóstrofe *s*.

    Ejemplos:
    someone **else's** problem
    mother-in-**law's** visit
    board of **directors'** policy
    Pope John Paul **II's** illness
    Proctor and **Gamble's** product
    Wayne and **Judy's** log cabin

- Palabras que muestran periodos de tiempo o cantidades de dinero necesitan apóstrofe cuando son usadas como adjetivos posesivos.

    Ejemplos:
    day's pay, **month's** vacation, **morning's** work
    two **cents'** worth, **dollar's** worth

- Un nombre singular que termina en *s* requiere el apóstrofe, a pesar de que muchos escritores quitan la *s* e incluyen solamente la apóstrofe.

    Ejemplos:
    Roger **Maris's** batting record
    Lotus's personal organizer

- Cuando un pronombre posesivo (*my, mine, ours, your, yours, his, her, hers, their, theirs*) es usado como adjetivo, no es necesario el uso del apóstrofe.

    Ejemplos:
    This is **their** idea. The idea is **theirs**.
    We filed **our** flight plan. The flight plan is **ours**.
    This manual must be **yours**.

PRÁCTICA

Elija la versión con la puntuación correcta de cada uno de los siguientes grupos de oraciones. Esté al tanto de lo que ha aprendido sobre el uso de la coma en la lección anterior.

1. a. An employee's motivation is different from an owner's.
   b. An employees' motivation is different from an owners'.

2. a. Employees reward's differ from an owners'.
   b. Employees' rewards differ from an owner's.

3. a. Elaine has worked three years as a physicians assistant.
   b. Elaine has worked three years as a physician's assistant.

4. a. The Mens' Issue's group meets every Saturday morning.
   b. The Men's Issues group meets every Saturday morning.

5. a. The companies' sales force has doubled in recent years, and the credit is your's.
   b. The company's sales force has doubled in recent years, and the credit is yours.

6. a. The most efficient method is her's.
   b. The most efficient method is hers.

7. a. After five years' experience, we earn four weeks' paid vacation.
   b. After five year's experience, we earn four week's paid vacation.

8. a. Pat and Janice's proposal requires a month's work.
   b. Pat's and Janice's proposal requires a months' work.

9. a. The computer supply store's top-selling printer is Hewlett Packards latest model.
   b. The computer supply store's top-selling printer is Hewlett Packard's latest model.

10. a. Ms. Jones's boutique sells the same products as Mr. Smith's.
   b. Ms. Jones' boutique sells the same products as Mr. Smiths'.

PARA DEMOSTRAR OMISIÓN

Use una apóstrofe para mostrar cuáles letras o números han sido omitidos.

Ejemplos:

> Morton **doesn't** (does not) live here anymore.
>
> The officer **couldn't** (could not) give me a speeding ticket.
>
> **Who's** (who is) on first?
>
> I just **can't** (cannot) understand this memo.
>
> The task force discussed the **nat'l** (national) debt.
>
> My first car was a **'67** (1967) Chevy.
>
> Grandpa tells stories about life in the **'40s** (1940s).

GUIONES

Un guión es una marca de puntuación muy especializada y reservada sólo para situaciones muy especiales. De todas maneras, muchos escritores lo usan incorrectamente en lugar de otras marcas de puntuación. Guiones llaman la atención del lector. Un escritor cuidadoso los tiene que usar cuidadosamente. Los guiones son muy eficaces si son usados correctamente, caso contrario, pierden su importancia.

Recuerde que tiene que diferenciar entre guiones y rayas cuando está escribiendo.

- Use una marca de guión para indicar una repentina interrupción de pensamiento o para añadir un comentario.

  Ejemplos:

  > Here is your sandwich and your—Look out for that bee!
  >
  > I remember the day—what middle-aged person doesn't—that President Kennedy was shot.
  >
  > John is sorry—we all are—about your unfortunate accident.

- Use una marca de guión para enfatizar información explicativa. No tiene que necesariamente usar guiones, pero puede hacerlo.

  Ejemplos:

  > Knowing yourself—your thoughts, values, and dreams—is the most important knowledge.
  >
  > "The writer is by nature a dreamer—a conscious dreamer." —*Carson McCullers*
  >
  > We spend our summers in Canada—Ontario, to be precise.

- Use una marca de guión para indicar letras o palabras omitidas.

  Ejemplo:

  > "Hello?—Yes, I can hear you just fine.—Of course—I think I can.—Good!—I'll see you later.—

- Use una marca de guión para conectar una frase inicial con el resto de la oración.

  Ejemplos:

  > Honesty, integrity, tenacity—these are marks of motivated salespeople.
  >
  > Nashville, Tennessee; Olympia, Washington; Osceola, Iowa—these are the prospective locations.

PRÁCTICA

Elija la opción en la cual los guiones y otras formas de puntuación son usadas correctamente en cada uno de los siguientes grupos.

11. a. We have only one choice—to open a new branch office in the suburbs.
   b. We have only one choice to open a new branch office—in the suburbs.

12. a. My suggestion—just in case you're interested, is to apply for a promotion.
   b. My suggestion—just in case you're interested—is to apply for a promotion.

13. a. He is the most unreasonable, I guess I should keep my opinions to myself.
   b. He is the most unreasonable—I guess I should keep my opinions to myself.

14. a. I can't find the pocket organizer that I worked—Oh, here it is.
   b. I can't find the pocket organizer that I worked, Oh, here it is.

15. a. Brains, brawn, determination—that's what I demand from my people.
   b. Brains, brawn, determination: that's what I demand from my people.

PRÁCTICA Y REPASO

Evalúese a sí mismo con las preguntas que siguen. Estas oraciones extremadamente difíciles cubren la materia que ha aprendido hasta ahora. Vea los grupos con mucho cuidado. ¿Cuál de las siguientes opciones ha sido escrita con la puntuación correcta?

16. a. Although it may seem strange, my partners purpose in interviewing Dr. E. S. Sanders Jr., was to eliminate him as a suspect in the crime.
   b. Although it may seem strange my partner's purpose in interviewing Dr. E. S. Sanders, Jr. was to eliminate him, as a suspect in the crime.
   c. Although it may seem strange, my partner's purpose in interviewing Dr. E. S. Sanders, Jr., was to eliminate him as a suspect in the crime.
   d. Although it may seem strange, my partner's purpose in interviewing Dr. E. S. Sanders, Jr. was to eliminate him, as a suspect in the crime.

17. a. After colliding with a vehicle at the intersection of Grand, and Forest Ms. Anderson saw a dark hooded figure reach through the window, grab a small parcel and run north on Forest.

b. After colliding with a vehicle at the intersection of Grand, and Forest, Ms. Anderson saw a dark hooded figure reach through the window, grab a small parcel, and run north on Forest.

c. After colliding with a vehicle at the intersection of Grand and Forest Ms. Anderson saw a dark, hooded figure reach through the window, grab a small parcel and run north on Forest.

d. After colliding with a vehicle at the intersection of Grand and Forest, Ms. Anderson saw a dark, hooded figure reach through the window, grab a small parcel, and run north on Forest.

18. a. When we interviewed each of the boys and the fathers, we determined that the men's stories did not match up with the boy's versions.

b. When we interviewed each of the boys and the fathers, we determined that the men's stories did not match up with the boys' versions.

c. When we interviewed each of the boys and the fathers, we determined that the mens' stories did not match up with the boys' versions.

d. When we interviewed each of the boy's and the father's, we determined that the men's stories did not match up with the boys' versions.

19. a. Bring these items when you drive up here tomorrow—Bobbys sleeping bag, another can of insect repellent, the girls queen-sized air mattress—they want to use it to sunbathe on the water, and my swimming trunks.

b. Bring these items when you drive up here tomorrow: Bobby's sleeping bag, another can of insect repellent, the girls' queen-sized air mattress—they want to use it to sunbathe on the water—and my swimming trunks.

c. Bring these items when you drive up here tomorrow: Bobby's sleeping bag, another can of insect repellent, the girl's queen-sized air mattress—they want to use it to sunbathe on the water, and my swimming trunks.

d. Bring these items when you drive up here tomorrow. Bobby's sleeping bag, another can of insect repellent, the girls queen-sized air mattress, they want to use it to sunbathe on the water, and my swimming trunks.

20. a. James Autry, Steven Covey, Madeline Hunter—these authors are responsible for my management style, a combination of Autry's personnel philosophy, Covey's process for prioritizing, and Hunter's organizational principles.

b. James Autry, Steven Covey, Madeline Hunter. These authors are responsible for my management style, a combination of Autry's personnel philosophy, Covey's process for prioritizing and Hunter's organizational principles.

c. James Autry, Steven Covey, Madeline Hunter—these authors are responsible for my management style, a combination of Autrys personnel philosophy, Coveys process for prioritizing and Hunters organizational principles.

d. James Autry, Steven Covey, Madeline Hunter: these authors are responsible for my management style; a combination of Autry's personnel philosophy; Covey's process for prioritizing; and Hunter's organizational principles.

Técnicas de aprendizaje

Muy poca gente entiende completamente las reglas para el uso de apóstrofes y guiones. Gente que trabaja en publicidad son notorios por usar incorrectamente ambos tipos de puntuación. Ponga atención especial a los anuncios y boletines publicitarios de los periódicos y revistas. Busque lugares en los cuales los apóstrofes y los guiones son usados correctamente. Note los lugares donde son omitidos o añadidos cuando no deberían serlo. Si su trabajo es aquél donde se produce materia de promoción, examine algunos de sus trabajos escritos para ver si apóstrofes y guiones han sido usados correctamente.

Respuestas

1. a.	**6.** b.	**11.** a.	**16.** c.
2. b.	**7.** a.	**12.** b.	**17.** d.
3. b.	**8.** a.	**13.** b.	**18.** b.
4. b.	**9.** b.	**14.** a.	**19.** b.
5. b.	**10.** a.	**15.** a.	**20.** a.

LAS COMILLAS

8

RESUMEN DE LA LECCIÓN

Esta lección cubre las reglas relacionadas con el uso de las comillas, dobles y simples. Pese a que estas marcas de puntuación generalmente se las encuentran en diálogos, son también importantes en otros modos de escritura.

Comience esta lección después de determinar lo mucho que usted ya sabe sobre el uso de comillas. Insértelas en las oraciones donde usted cree que son necesarias usando la columna **Problema** de la página que sigue. Revise y compare sus respuestas con las oraciones de la columna **Solución**.

Problema	Solución
Into the shelter yelled the captain.	"Into the shelter!" yelled the captain.
My first personal essay was called My Life and Death.	My first personal essay was called "My Life and Death."
William Hickock richly deserved the name Wild Bill.	William Hickock richly deserved the name "Wild Bill."
I wish that old fussbudget— Melanie stopped abruptly as Mr. Harris walked into the room.	"I wish that old fussbudget—" Melanie stopped abruptly as Mr. Harris walked into the room.
None of us had heard of halupsi before.	None of us had heard of "halupsi" before.
If we don't hurry said Jack we'll be late for the show.	"If we don't hurry," said Jack, "we'll be late for the show."
Why are you still here my supervisor asked. Everyone else went home an hour ago.	"Why are you still here?" my supervisor asked. "Everyone else went home an hour ago."
I read the editorial called Big Boys in Washington.	I read the editorial called "Big Boys in Washington."
You've said actually twelve times in the past two minutes.	You've said "actually" twelve times in the past two minutes.
David said The customer said No way before I ever had a chance to explain.	David said, "The customer said, 'No way!' before I ever had a chance to explain."
We matted and framed a print of Woodland Tide and hung it on the office wall.	We matted and framed a print of "Woodland Tide" and hung it on the office wall.
Our Christmas bonus was a bag with a cookie and an orange.	Our Christmas "bonus" was a bag with a cookie and an orange.
With his tardy record, I can see why you refer to him as Punctual Paul.	With his tardy record, I can see why you refer to him as "Punctual Paul."

LAS COMILLAS Y LAS CITAS DIRECTAS

■ Use comillas para establecer una cita directa o un pensamiento en una oración o párrafo. Esto incluye citas que son firmadas, inscritas, grabadas, y otras más.

Ejemplos:

Mr. Hurley called our prototype "a model of pure genius."

I was certain he said, "Campbells will accept delivery on Tuesday."

"When will help arrive?" I wondered.

The sign clearly read, "No trespassing or hunting."

"Happy and Fulfilled," the headstone read.

■ No use comillas en paráfrasis o citas indirectas.

Ejemplos:

I was sure Campbells wanted a Tuesday delivery.

I wondered when help would arrive.

The sign said that trespassing and hunting were not allowed.

■ Uso de comillas simples para establecer una cita dentro de otra.

Ejemplos:

"I distinctly heard her say, 'The store opens at 9:00.'" said Gene.

The speaker continued, "I am ever mindful of Franklin Roosevelt's famous words, 'We have nothing to fear but fear itself.' But fear is a terrible thing."

My speech teacher asked, "Does anyone in this room remember the way Jim Nabors used to say, 'Golly'?"

UNAS PALABRAS SOBRE DIÁLOGO

El uso de puntuación correcta en un diálogo significa entender como usar comillas, comas, y símbolos finales de puntuación. En el ejemplo que sigue, examine de cerca las oraciones, las mismas que incluyen estructuras básicas de diálogo. Las palabras citadas son denominadas *citas*, y las palabras que explican quién dijo la citas son conocidas como *citas*. En el ejemplo que sigue, las *citas* han sido marcados.

1. "I'm really thirsty. Let's grab something to drink," **said Horace.**

2. **Nancy replied,** "I'm thirsty, but I don't have any cash. Do you have some?"

3. "I don't get it," **Horace answered.** "You're the manager with the high-paying job."

4. "Well," **Nancy replied,** "credit cards are all I ever use."

Palabras citadas siempre van acompañadas por comillas. Ponga las comillas delante de un grupo de palabras citadas y luego al final de las mismas.

Las *citas* son usados de diferente forma dependiendo en dónde están ubicados dentro de una oración. Cada vez que una *cita* sigue una cita, y la misma es una oración que normalmente termina con un punto final, use una coma al final de la oración. El punto final debe colocarse al final de la cita. De otra forma, si la cita es una oración que normalmente termina con un signo de interrogación o exclamación, ponga dicho signo de puntuación al final de la cita. Coloque un punto final después de la cita. (Vea oración 1 en la página 73.)

> "I'm really thirsty. Let's grab something to drink," said Alvina.
> "I'm really thirsty. Do you want to grab something to drink?" asked Alvina.
> "I'm really thirsty. Hold it—a Dairy Queen!" exclaimed Alvina.

A veces, el comando precede la cita. Cuando esto pasa, ponga una coma después de la cita. Ponga comillas fuera de la palabras citadas, escriba en mayúsculas la primera palabra de la cita, y use la puntuación adecuada. (Vea oración 2 en la página 73.)

A veces el comando interrumpe la cita. Si ambas partes de una cita, la primera y la segunda, son oraciones completas, la primera parte de la cita usa la puntuación que se usaría cuando una cita tiene la cita al final. En otras palabras, el punto final sigue a la cita. El resto de la cita usa puntuación de la misma manera que una cita precedida por una cita. (Vea oración 3 en la página 73.)

Cuando la cita interrumpe la cita y la oración, las palabras que preceden a la cita comienzan la idea, y las palabras que siguen a la cita terminan la idea. Ponga una coma después de la cita (no un punto final, ya que la oración no está completa). Ponga las comillas alrededor de la última parte de la cita, pero no ponga en mayúsculas la primera letra de la cita. No es el comienzo de una oración. Para el resto de la oración, use elementos de puntuación que normalmente usaría. (Vea oración 4 en la página 73.)

NOTA: Toda la puntuación está ubicada **internamente** dentro de las comillas, menos las marcas de puntuación que siguen a las citas.

Diálogo en breve

- Tag following the quotation mark:
    "—————," said Rose.
    "—————?" asked Rose.
    "—————!" exclaimed Rose.
- Tag preceding quotation:
    Iris said, "—————."
    Iris asked, "—————?"
    Iris exclaimed, "—————!"
- Tag between two sentences of a quotation:
    "—————," said Lily. "—————."
    "—————?" asked Lily. "—————?"
    "—————!" exclaimed Lily. "—————!"

■ Tag interrupting a quotation and a sentence:

"————," said Daisy, "————."

"————," asked Daisy, "————?"

"————," exclaimed Daisy, "————!"

OTROS USOS DE LAS COMILLAS

■ Use comillas para enfatizar palabras no familiares o apodos. A veces las comillas son usadas para referirse a palabras que describen otras palabras, aunque muy a menudo, usted verá esas palabras en letras itálicas .

Ejemplos:

None of us had heard of "chutney" before we read the article.

He was dubbed "Sir Tagalong" by the other members of the staff.

The Scrabble players disagreed over the term "ptu." (or " . . . over the term *ptu*.")

■ Use comillas para indicar algo irónico o que llame la atención. Pero no abuse del uso de las comillas en esta forma; no siempre funcionará si lo hace muy a menudo.

Ejemplos:

When we were camping, our "bathroom" was a thicket behind our tent.

Our "guide" never mentioned la presence of poison ivy.

The "fun" of surgery begins long before the operation commences.

■ Use comillas para diferenciar títulos u otros factores. Otros títulos deben ser subrayados o puestos en itálicas.

Dentro de las comillas	Subrayardo o en itálicas
nombre de una historia o capítulo de un libro	título de un libro
nombre de un programa de televisión	nombre de una película
título de un poema	título de una colección de poesía o un poema épico
título de un artículo o un reporte	nombre de una revista o un periódico
título de una canción	título de un musical, obra de teatro, o composición musicas
	Nombre de un barco, avión o tren, etc.

PUNTUACIÓN DENTRO DE LAS COMILLAS

Estas son las reglas relacionadas con el uso de otros signos de puntuación y las comillas.

■ Signos de interrogación, admiración, y guiones van dentro de las comillas siempre y cuando éstos sean parte de las cita. Si no lo son, póngalas fuera de las comillas.

Ejemplos:

The doctor asked, "Can you feel any pain in this area?" [Part of the quotation]

Have you read Nathaniel Hawthorne's "The Birthmark"? [Not part of the quotation]

"I wish I'd never heard of—" Karen stopped abruptly as Nick walked in the room. [Part of the quotation]

"Stage left," "stage right," "upstage," and "downstage"—I always confused these terms. [Not part of the quotation]

- Puntos finales y comas van **adentro** de las comillas.

    "Let's wait a few minutes," suggested Doris, "before we leave."

- Dos puntos y punto y comas van **afuera** de las comillas.

    I can see only one challenge for the speaker of "The Road Less Traveled": ambivalence.

    The critic called the latest sculpture an "abomination to sensitive eyes"; the artist was hurt.

PRÁCTICA

Elija la forma correcta de puntuación en cada una de las siguientes oraciones. Revise el uso de comillas como también otros elementos generales de puntuación.

1. a. "Have you ever read the story 'The Open Window' by O. Henry? asked Martha.

  b. "Have you ever read the story 'The Open Window' by O. Henry?" asked Martha.

  c. "Have you ever read the story "The Open Window" by O. Henry?" asked Martha.

2. a. Did you know it was Winston Churchill who called Russia "a riddle wrapped up in a mystery inside an enigma"?

  b. Did you know it was "Winston Churchill" who called Russia "a riddle wrapped up in a mystery inside an enigma?"

  c. Did you know it was Winston Churchill who called Russia "a riddle wrapped up in a mystery inside an enigma?"

3. a. After reading a review of Toy Story, I wanted to see the movie.

  b. After reading a review of <u>Toy Story</u>, I wanted to see the movie.

  c. After reading a review of "Toy Story," I wanted to see the movie.

4. a. Leaving five minutes early on Friday was our "reward."

  b. Leaving five minutes early on Friday was our "reward".

  c. Leaving five minutes early on Friday was our 'reward.'

5. a. "Megabyte," "baud speed," "internal RAM"—these are all examples of technical terms.

  b. "Megabyte," "baud speed," "internal RAM—" these are all examples of technical terms.

  c. "Megabyte", "baud speed", "internal RAM"—these are all examples of technical terms.

6. a. If you read my article Budget Play in this morning's <u>Register</u>, you'll understand why I'm so cynical about Washington politicians.

    b. If you read my article "Budget Play" in this morning's "Register", you'll understand why I'm so cynical about Washington politicians.

    c. If you read my article "Budget Play" in this morning's <u>Register</u>, you'll understand why I'm so cynical about Washington politicians.

7. a. "The story 'What Does Anyone Really Understand?' certainly gave me something to think about," remarked Uncle Art.

    b. 'The story "What Does Anyone Really Understand?" certainly gave me something to think about,' remarked Uncle Art.

    c. "The story "What Does Anyone Really Understand?" certainly gave me something to think about," remarked Uncle Art.

8. a. "Do you name all your cats Howard," asked my friend Ted.

    b. "Do you name all your cats Howard"? asked my friend Ted.

    c. "Do you name all your cats Howard?" asked my friend Ted.

9. a. The officer asked us whether we had seen the accident.

    b. The officer asked us whether we had seen the accident?

    c. The officer asked us, "Whether we had seen the accident."

10. a. "You would be better off not to offer any excuses," the personnel director advised, "I'm afraid that will only make matters worse."

    b. "You would be better off not to offer any excuses." the personnel director advised. "I'm afraid that will only make matters worse."

    c. "You would be better off not to offer any excuses," the personnel director advised. "I'm afraid that will only make matters worse."

Técnicas de aprendizaje

Busque ejemplos del uso de citas en todo lo que lea. Cuando las encuentre vea si las han usado correctamente.

RESPUESTAS

1. b.

2. a.

3. b.

4. a.

5. a.

6. c.

7. a.

8. c.

9. a.

10. c.

L · E · C · C · I · Ó · N
PUNTUACIÓN MÁS AVANZADA
9

RESUMEN DE LA LECCIÓN

Esta lección cubre algunas de las menos usadas formas de puntuación incluyendo guiones, paréntesis, barras, elipsis, y líneas diagonales. Pese a que estos signos de puntuación no se presentan muy a menudo, es preciso saber como usarlos correctamente.

Las formas de puntuación más comunes que se estudiarán en esta lección—guiones, paréntesis, barras, elipsis, y líneas diagonales—no son muy comunmente usadas en la escritura regular. De todas maneras, tienen y sirven funciones bien específicas. Conocerlas y entenderlas ofrece ventajas para el escritor. Debido a que estas reglas son bastante especializadas, ya que muy poca gente las conoce, empezaremos directamente con la lección en lugar de hacer una evaluación inicial. La última parte de esta lección explica cómo usar números en su forma escrita.

GUIONES

El propósito principal de un guión (-) es unir palabras para crear nombres o adjetivos compuestos. Guiones señalan palabras que trabajan juntas para un determinado propósito.

Nombres compuestos pueden ser escritos como palabras independientes, como dos palabras, o como palabras unidas por guiones. Cuando usted dude de su uso consulte con un diccionario. Ya que el idioma cambia constantemente, estas palabras también evolucionan en su significado. Una palabra compuesta, escrita como dos palabras puede ser escrita como una palabra que lleva guiones, y luego puede ser escrita como una simple palabra. Como por ejemplo, la palabra *semicolon* se escribía como dos palabras separadas: *semi colon*. A finales de los años cincuenta, diccionarios empezaron a anotar y escribir esta palabra con un guión entre medio. En un diccionario reciente la palabra aparece como: *semicolon*.

Palabras simples compuestas	**Dos palabras compuestas**	**Nombres compuestos con uso del guión**
tablecloth	parking lot	
horsefly	couch potato	jack-in-the-box
textbook	floppy disk	brother-in-law
catwalk		money-maker
bedroom		city-state
		well-being
		merry-go-round

- Use un guión para unir dos nombres iguales que dentro de una oración trabajen como uno solo.

  Shannon is a **teacher-poet.**

  Pete Rose was a **player-coach** for the Cincinnati Reds.

  Kevin Costner has joined the ranks of well-known **actor-directors.**

- Use un guión para unir muchas palabras compuestas.

  fly-by-night, stick-in-the-mud, good-for-nothing, three-year-old

- Use un guión para unir dos o mas palabras que funcionan como adjetivos independientes que *preceden* al nombre.

  The hikers saw a **run-down** cabin in the clearing.

  Much has been written about the **Kennedy-Nixon** debates.

  An **ill-trained** police officer is more of a menace than protector.

  The company employed a **high-powered** consultant.

  A **soft-spoken** answer to the angry accusation ended the disagreement.

  His **off-the-wall** remarks keep our meetings lively and interesting.

  The parties finally agreed after three months of **hard-nosed** negotiations.

  A **French-Canadian** bicyclist won the **three-week** race.

- Si las palabras que están funcionando como adjetivos independientes *siguen* al nombre, éstas no deben ser unidas por un guión.

  The cabin the hikers saw in the clearing was **run down.**

  A police officer who is **ill trained** is more of a menace than a protector.

  The consultant employed by the company was **high powered.**

  The parties finally agreed after three months of negotiations that were **hard nosed.**

- Use un guión para unir a las palabras prefijos como; *self, half, ex, all, great, post, pro,* y *vice* o los sufijos *elect*.

  Harry Truman unleashed the **all-powerful** atomic weapon.

  Abraham Lincoln was a **self-made** man.

  Keep your **half-baked** ideas to yourself.

  Simone spotted her **ex-husband** walking into the grocery store.

  My **great-grandfather** turns 102 next Wednesday.

  Many remember the **post-WWII** years with great fondness.

  Conservatives consider the front-runner to be a **pro-abortion** candidate.

  The **secretary-elect** picked up all the records from the presiding secretary.

- Use un guión para evitar confusión o con ortografía rara.

  The coach decided to **re-pair** [rather than repair] the debate partners.

  The neighbors decided to **re-cover** [rather than recover] their old sofa.

  The sculpture had a **bell-like** [rather than belllike] shape.

- Use un guión para unir una mayúscula a una palabra.

  The **U-joint** went out in our second car.

  The architect worked with nothing more than a **T-square**.

- Use un guión para escribir cifras de dos palabras entre el 21 y 99.

  twenty-six, thirty-three, sixty-four, seventy-two, ninety-nine

- Use un guión para unir fracciones escritas en palabras.

  three-fifths, five-sixteenths, five thirty-seconds

- Use un guión para unir números con palabras usadas como adjetivos independientes.

  three-yard pass, eight-inch steel, two-word sentence, five-stroke lead

NOTA: Cuando en una oración se escribe una serie de adjetivos numéricos, use la combinación de guión y coma con todas las partes de la serie menos la última.

  Precut particle board comes in **two-, four-,** and **six-foot** squares.

  Andy scored three touchdowns on **eight-, fourteen-,** and **two-yard** runs.

- Use un guión para unir números y adjetivos.

  fifty-four-year-old woman, ten-dollar profit, two-thousand-acre ranch, twenty-minute wait

- Use un guión para escribir en palabras la hora del día.

  twelve-thirty, four-o'clock appointment, six-fifteen A.M., one-fifty-five in the morning

- Use un guión para unir números que indican tiempo de vida, puntaje, o la duración de un evento.

  Abraham Lincoln (**1809-65**) served as the sixteenth President, **1861-65**.

  The Cowboys beat the Eagles **21-3**.

- Use un guión para separar una palabra de entre medio de sílabas al final de una oración. Estas son algunas de las reglas para dividir palabras.

  Nunca deje en una sílaba una letra independiente en una línea.

  Divida palabras unidas por guiones en el guión.

  Nunca divida una palabra de una sola sílaba.

Evite dividir palabras que tengan menos de seis letras.

Evite dividir la última palabra de un párrafo.

Evite dividir los números.

CONSULTE SIEMPRE CON UN DICCIONARIO SI ES QUE TIENE DUDAS.

PARÉNTESIS

- Use paréntesis para incluir material de explicación que interrumpe el flujo normal de oraciones y está relacionado al texto solo marginalmente.

    Thirty-sixth Street (a party street if there ever was one) is a fun place to live.

    Our neighbors threw a huge party on New Year's Eve. (Fortunately, we were invited.)

    Unfortunately, another set of neighbors (they were not invited) called the police to complain about the noise.

    We party-goers (how were we to know?) were completely surprised by the officers.

Observe las últimas tres oraciones. Cada grupo de paréntesis contiene una oración completa. Si la construcción de paréntesis está ubicada al final de la oración, ésta tiene que ser escrita como tal dentro de su propio paréntesis. Por otro lado, si está en una oración diferente, mayúsculas y puntos apartes no son necesarios. De todas maneras, si la construcción de paréntesis en el centro de otra oración es una oración que normalmente requiere un signo de interrogación o exclamación, incluya esta puntuación.

- Use paréntesis para incluir información cuando es necesario escribir con exactitud.

    The two sons of Richard Hannika (Scott and William) are sole heirs to his fortune.

    We hereby agree to sell the heirloom for sixty-three dollars ($63.00).

- Use paréntesis para incluir letras o números que marcan una división.

    This lesson includes several little-used, often-misused punctuation marks: (a) hyphens, (b) parentheses, (c) brackets, (d) diagonals, and (e) ellipses.

    Your task consists of three steps: (1) locating information, (2) writing a report, and (3) delivering a presentation about your findings.

BARRAS

- Use barras para incluir material en paréntesis dentro de paréntesis.

    Brandi planned to work as an aeronautic engineer (she completed an internship at National Aeronautics and Space Administration [NASA]) as soon as she completed her doctoral work.

■ Use barras para incluir palabras añadidas en una cita.

"The next head nurse [Shawna DeWitt] will face the challenge of operating the floor with a reduced staff."

■ Use barras con la palabra *sic* para demostrar que un error en una cita ha sido cometido por el escritor u orador original.

"Unless we heel [sic] the nation's economic woes, social problems will continue to mount."

ELIPSES

Los puntos de elipses se asemejan a los puntos finales pero no funcionan como éstos. Escriba tres puntos para formar elipses. Estas marcas indican material omitido o pausas largar.

■ Use elipses para mostrar que material citado ha sido omitido. Si la omisión es al final de la oración, escriba un punto final despues de las elipses.

"Four-score and seven years ago … equal."

"We hold these truths to be self-evident…."

■ Use elipses para indicar una pausa o duda.

And the winner for "Best Actor" is … Dustin Hoffman.

I think that adds up to … exactly eighty-three dollars.

LÍNEAS DIAGONALES

Al igual que los guiones, una línea diagonal es una marca para unir palabras o números. El uso más común de líneas diagonales es con la frase *and/or* que muestra que la oración se refiere a una o ambas de las palabras unidas.

For breakfast we can make bacon and/or French toast.

Vinegar and/or egg whites added to plain water will make an excellent hair rinse that leaves hair soft and silky.

■ Use línea diagonal para separar números de fracciones.

Normally, it takes us 3 1/2 hours to sort the bulk mail at the end of the week.

You'll need a 1 5/8-inch wrench for this nut.

■ Use línea diagonal para mostrar divisiones de líneas en poesía.

"Goodnight, goodnight, parting is such sweet sorrow / That I shall say good night 'till it be morrow. / Sleep dwell upon thine eyes and peace in thy breast! / Would I were sleep and peace so sweet to rest!"

■ Use línea diagonal para indicar *per* o *divided by*.

The cars in the new fleet average over 25 miles/gallon.

Shares are calculated in this way: net profit/number of shareholders.

NÚMEROS

Son pocas las reglas que rigen el uso de números en la escritura. En periodismo, se prefiere escribir las cifras ya que son fáciles de identificar y leer. De todas maneras, un número que comienza una oración está siempre escrito en palabras. Para escribir más formalmente, siga las convenciones establecidas en la siguiente página.

- Use números arábigos en lugar de romanos: *1, 2, 3, 4* en lugar de *I, II, III, IV.*
- Si un número puede ser escrito como una o dos palabras, escribalo como palabra. Caso contrario, escriba la cifra: *8, twenty-six, 124, three hundred, 8,549, five million.*
- Siempre escriba en palabras los números al principio de una oración incluso si es más de dos palabras.

PRÁCTICA

En las siguientes oraciones, añada guiones donde sean necesarios.

1. According to your brain X rays, I see little justification for you to act like a know it all.

2. Father Tan, now an ex priest, reevaluated his theology and became a pro life activist.

3. Syheed's well grounded arguments impressed the crowd of forty five.

4. Ned's time in the four hundred meter freestyle was twenty seven hundredths of a second off the world record time.

5. Following a two hour business venture involving a lemonade stand, the ten year old boy had made a five dollar and fifty cent profit.

En las siguientes oraciones añada guiones, paréntesis, barras, elipses, y líneas diagonales donde sean necesarias.

6. Muhammad Ali few people remember him as Cassius Clay wrote a poem describing himself as someone who could "… float like a butterflie sic, sting like a bee."

7. Year end bonuses will come in the form of dollars and or vacation days for about three fifths 3 5 of our staff.

8. Before leaving today, please 1 collect the latest sales data 2 add up all the figures and 3 leave them in my left hand drawer.

Técnicas de aprendizaje

Hoy, mientras usted lee, busque ejemplos de los signos de puntuación estudiados en esta lección. Como éstos son usados con menos frecuencia, quizá no los vea muy a menudo. Cuando los encuentre trate de recordar como fueron escritos. Esté al tanto especialmente en anuncios publicitarios del uso de guiones, paréntesis, barras, lineas diagonales, y elipses; vea si han sido usados correctamente.

RESPUESTAS

1. According to your brain X-rays, I see little justification for you to act like a know-it-all.
2. Father Tan, now an ex-priest, re-evaluated his theology and became a pro-life activist.
3. Syheed's well-grounded arguments impressed the crowd of forty-five.
4. Ned's time in the four-hundred-meter freestyle was twenty-seven-hundredths of a second off the world record time.
5. Following a two-hour business venture involving a lemonade stand, the ten-year-old boy had made a five-dollar and fifty-cent profit.
6. Muhammad Ali (few people remember him as Cassius Clay) wrote a poem describing himself as someone who could "… float like a butterflie [sic], sting like a bee."
7. Year-end bonuses will come in the form of dollars and/or vacation days for about three-fifths (3/5) of our staff.
8. Before leaving today, please (1) collect the latest sales data, (2) add up all the figures, and (3) leave them in my left-hand drawer.

L · E · C · C · I · Ó · N

TIEMPO DE LOS VERBOS

10

RESUMEN DE LA LECCIÓN

Los verbos—palabras que describen acciones o estados de ánimo—son los motores principales que dan vida al lenguaje escrito. Debido a su importancia, errores que involucran el uso de verbos son muy notables. Esos errores son los que generalmente se presentan en exámenes de pruebas civiles. Esta lección, así como la próximas dos que siguen, le ayudarán a evitar algunos de los errores más comunes en el uso de verbos.

Escritores usan palabras para establecer su credibilidad. Pocas son las cosas que causan la duda sobre la destreza de un escritor como el mal uso de palabras—especialmente verbos. Formas verbales incorrectas llaman mucho la atención a sí mismas y ponen en duda la educación e inteligencia del escritor. Por otro lado, los exámenes de prueba civil generalmente evaluan su conocimiento del uso de verbos y cómo éstos pueden ser evadidos.

Esta lección explica como usar verbos correctamente y señala algunos de los errores más comunes que cometen los escritores. En la siguiente página, vea cuántos de los siete errores verbales usted puede encontrar en la versión **Problema**. En la columna **Solución**, el párrafo está escrito con la forma verbal correcta. A medida que usted avance la lección, trate de aplicar las reglas aprendidas en esas correcciones.

Problema

When I was sixteen, my grandmother gave me an heirloom ring that her grandmother had gave her. It was a polished garnet set in hammered silver with two rubies on either side of it. I could of sold it for a small fortune last week. An antique dealer come through town and heard about my ring. He asks to see it. His eyes nearly popped out of his head as he examined it. If I wasn't such a sentimental person, I might have parted with it. But a treasure like that wasn't something you should sell.

Solución

When I was sixteen, my grandmother gave me an heirloom ring that her grandmother had given her. It is a polished garnet set in hammered silver with two rubies on either side of it. I could have sold it for a small fortune last week. An antique dealer came through town and heard about my ring. He asked to see it. His eyes nearly popped out of his head as he examined it. If I weren't such a sentimental person, I might have parted with it. But a treasure like that isn't something you should sell.

PARTES PRINCIPALES DE UN VERBO

Los verbos tienen tres partes principales:

- **Presente**—la forma del verbo que complementaría la oración, "Today, I _____."
- **Pasado**—la forma del verbo que complementaría la oración, "Yesterday, I _____."
- **Participio Pasado**—la forma del verbo que complementaría la oración, "Often, I have _____."

Para la mayor parte de los verbos, es fácil crear las tres partes principales si usted sabe la forma en el presente. Tome como ejemplo el verbo "look." *Today, I look. Yesterday I looked. Often, I have looked.* Para verbos regulares, ambas formas del pasado y del participio pasado, añaden *d* o *-ed* a la forma del presente. Pero el idioma inglés está lleno de verbos irregulares que forman sus pasados y participios pasados de otras maneras. La tabla en la página 87, muestra las partes principales de muchos de los verbos que son generalmente mal usados.

PRÁCTICA

En cada una de las siguientes oraciones, encierre en un círculo la forma correcta del verbo. Las respuestas pueden ser encontradas al final de la lección.

1. The team has certainly (do, did, done) a good job on this presentation.

2. The sales clerk just (throw, threw, thrown) away the opportunity to make a huge commission.

3. The senator (speak, spoke, spoken) at the press conference last Monday.

4. The phone has (ring, rang, rung) only once today.

TRES PARTES PRINCIPALES VERBALES		
Presente	**Pasado**	**Participio Pasado***
do	did	done
go	went	gone
see	saw	seen
drink	drank	drunk
break	broke	broken
bring	brought	brought
choose	chose	chosen
know	knew	known
wear	wore	worn
write	wrote	written

* Nota: Las conjugaciones en participio pasado deben ser precedidas por las palabras have, has, *o* had.

5. The speaker (come, came) to the point very early in the speech.

6. Harriet (see, saw, seen) the prototype for the new product at the convention.

7. The company has not yet (begin, began, begun) to manufacture its most current model.

8. Has the admitting staff (go, went, gone) to lunch?

9. Heather lost a filling when she (bite, bit, bitten) into the piece of hard candy.

10. Ben couldn't believe that someone had actually (steal, stole, stolen) his car from the ramp.

EL USO CONSISTENTE DE TIEMPO VERBAL

El tiempo de un verbo nos dice cuando la acción ocurre, ocurrió, o va a ocurrir. Los verbos tienen tres conjugaciones básicas: presente, pasado, y futuro. Mientras escribe, es importante mantener consistencia en las conjugaciones verbales. Un párrafo que comienza con la conjugación en presente, debe continuar en presente. Si comienza en pasado, debe de mantenerse en pasado. No mezcle conjugaciones.

Incorrecto:
    Dan **opened** the car door and **looks** for his briefcase.
Correcto:
    Dan **opened** the car door and **looked** for his briefcase.

Incorrecto:

When we **increase** maintenance services, we **reduced** repair costs.

Correcto:

When we **increase** maintenance services, we **reduce** repair costs.

Muchas veces un escritor debe mostrar que una acción ocurrió en otro tiempo sin importarle en qué tiempo se comenzó a escribir el párrafo. Para poder hacer esto, cada una de estas oraciones tiene tres sub-divisiones: progresiva, perfecta, y progresiva perfecta.

FORMAS DEL TIEMPO PRESENTE

El **tiempo presente** muestra acciones que pasan ahora o una acción que pasa muy a menudo. El **presente progresivo** muestra una acción que está ocurriendo ahora. El verbo auxiliar (*am, is, are*) precede la forma *-ing* (forma progresiva) del verbo. El **presente perfecto** muestra una acción que comenzó en el pasado. El verbo auxiliar *have* o *has* precede la forma del participio pasado del verbo. El **presente perfecto progresivo** también muestra una acción que comenzó en el pasado y está continuando en el presente. Los verbos auxiliares (*have been* o *has been*) preceden el verbo escrito en su forma *-ing* (forma progresiva).

TIEMPO PRESENTE			
Presente	**Progresivo**	**Perfecto**	**Progresivo perfecto**
muestra acción que está pasando ahora	muestra acción que está continuando ahora	muestra acción que comenzó en el pasado	muestra acción que comenzó en el pasado, y que ahora continua
Activists *lobby* for change.	Activists *are lobbying* for change.	Activists *have lobbied* for change.	Activists *have been lobbying* for change.
Sulfur *pollutes* the air.	Sulfur *is polluting* the air.	Sulfur *has polluted* the air.	Sulfur *has been polluting* the air.

Todas las formas del tiempo presente pueden ser usadas conjuntamente en una oración sin llegar a constituir un cambio en el tiempo de la oración. Observe el párrafo que sigue para que vea como funciona. Los verbos han sido marcados, y las barras identifican el tiempo de los verbos.

I **am writing** [present progressive] to protest the condition of the Mississippi River, from which our city **draws** [present] its drinking water. For years industrial waste **has polluted** [present perfect] its waters, and officials **pay** [present] little attention to the problem. People who live near the river **have been lobbying** [present perfect progressive] for protective legislation, but their efforts **have failed** [present perfect]. I **want** [present] safe water to drink.

FORMAS DEL TIEMPO PASADO

El **tiempo pasado** muestra una acción que ocurrió en el pasado. Usa la forma pasada del verbo. El **pasado progresivo** muestra una acción continua en el pasado. El verbo auxiliar *was* o *were* precede la forma progresiva *(-ing)* del verbo. El **pasado perfecto** muestra una acción completada en el pasado o completada antes de otra acción en el pasado. El verbo auxiliar *had* precede la forma del participio pasado. El **pasado perfecto progresivo** muestra la continuación de una acción iniciada en el pasado. El verbo auxiliar *had been* precede la forma progresiva del verbo.

TIEMPO PASADO			
Past	**Progresivo**	**Perfecto**	**Perfecto progresivo**
ocurrió en el pasado	acción que continua en el pasado	completado antes de otra acción	acción continuada que comenzó en el pasado
Local officials *spoke* to the management.	Local officials *were speaking* to the management.	Local officials *had spoken* to the management.	Local officials *had been speaking* to the management.
The reporter *covered* the meetings.	The reporter *was covering* the meetings.	The reporter *had covered* the meetings.	The reporter *had been covering* the meetings.

Todas las formas del tiempo pasado pueden ser usadas conjuntamente en una oración sin llegar a constituir un cambio en el tiempo de la oración. Observe el párrafo que sigue para que vea como funciona. Los verbos han sido marcados, y las barras identifican el tiempo de los verbos.

Last year, local officials **cited** [past] a manufacturing company in our county for improperly disposing of hazardous waste. The company **ignored** [past] the action and **continued** [past] to dump its waste as they **had been doing.** [past perfect progressive] They **had dumped** [past perfect] waste the same way for years and **planned** [past] to continue. Several months later the residue **seeped** [past] into the drinking water supply. A local environmentalist, who **had been tracking** [past perfect progressive] the company's dumping procedures, alerted local officials. They fined the company $3,000 for damages, but the company **has** never **paid** [past perfect] the fine.

FORMAS DEL TIEMPO FUTURO

El **tiempo futuro** muestra acción que todavía no ha llegado a ocurrir. Los verbos auxiliares *will, would,* o *shall* preceden la forma presente del verbo. El **futuro progresivo** muestra acciones continuas en el futuro. Las frases verbales auxiliares *will be, shall be,* o *would be* preceden la forma progresiva del verbo. El **futuro perfecto** muestra acciones que van a ser completadas en cierto tiempo en el futuro. Las frases auxiliares verbales *will have, would have,* o *will have been* preceden la forma del pasado participio del verbo. El **futuro perfecto progresivo** muestra acciones continuas que van a ser completadas en cierto tiempo en el futuro. Las frases verbales *will have been, would have been,* o *shall have been* preceden la forma progresiva del verbo.

Todas las formas del tiempo futuro de la tabla que sigue en la próxima página pueden ser usadas conjuntamente en una oración sin llegar a constituir un cambio en el tiempo de la oración. El párrafo que sigue demuestra como funciona. Los verbos han sido marcados, y las barras identifican el tiempo de los verbos.

TIEMPO FUTURO			
Futuro	**Progresivo**	**Perfecto**	**Progresivo perfecto**
acción que va a ocurrir	acción contínua que va a ocurrir	acción que va a ser completada en un cierto tiempo	acción contínua que será completada en un cierto tiempo
We *will begin* a letter-writing campaign.	Everyone *will be writing* letters.	By summer, we *will have written* reams of letters.	Legislators *will have been receiving* letters throughout the year.
Newspapers *will cover* this case.	Newspapers *will be covering* this case.	By summer, every newspaper *will have written* about this case.	Newspapers *will have been covering* the case throughout the year.

Starting next week, we **will reduce** [future] the money we spend on waste disposal. We **will do** [future] this because our public relations costs have skyrocketed during the year. Since no one in the community **will sell** [future] land to us to use for waste disposal, we **will be relocating** [future progressive] in a new community with a better business environment. This move **would put** [future] over three hundred employees out of work. It **would reduce** [future] the amount of consumer dollars spent at local businesses.

By this time next year, nearly one thousand people **will have lost** [future perfect] their jobs. Your business leaders **will have been looking** [future perfect progressive] for ways to replace lost revenue. Furthermore, legislators **will be meddling** [future progressive] in our local affairs, and the news media **will have portrayed** [future perfect] us all as fools.

COMO LOS TIEMPOS VERBALES COMUNICAN SIGNIFICADO

El manejar bien los tiempos verbales le ayuda al escritor evitar la confusión que viene con el descuido. Los siguientes ejemplos muestran cómo el tiempo verbal puede cambiar por completo el sentido de la oración.

Ejemplos:

Beth discovered that Nick had left work and gone home.

Beth discovered that Nick had left work and went home.

En la primera oración, ya que *gone* es la forma del participio, ésta va con *had left* en la segunda parte de la oración. Es Nick quien *had gone* a casa. En la segunda oración, *went* está en el pasado simple como *discovered* lo está en la primera parte de la oración. Entonces esta vez es Beth quien *went* a casa.

Ejemplos:

Cory told the officer that she had answered the phone and drank a can of soda pop.

Cory told the officer that she had answered the phone and had drunk a can of soda pop.

En la primera oración, *drank* está en el mismo tiempo que *told*—ambas están en tiempo pasado. Entonces Cory estaba tomando a la misma vez que estaba diciendo. En la segunda oración, *had drunk* iguala a *had answered*, entonces en este caso Cory estaba tomando cuando contestó el teléfono.

HAVE, Y NO *OF*

Al formar las diversas oraciones del tiempo perfecto, a veces la gente escribe *of* cuando deben escribir *have,* eso se debe probablemente a que escriben lo que escuchan. *I should've* (*should've* es una contracción de *should have*) suena mucho como *I should of.* Pero la manera correcta de escribirlo es *have* y no *of.*

Incorrecto:

I **could of** seen the difference if I had looked more closely.

Correcto:

I **could have** seen the difference if I had looked more closely.

Incorrecto:

The park ranger **should of** warned the campers about the bears.

Correcto:

The park ranger **should have** warned the campers about the bears.

CAMBIANDO TIEMPOS VERBALES

A veces uno tiene que cambiar del pasado al presente para evitar sugerir una mentira.

Incorrecto:

I met the new technician. He **was** very personable. [What happened? Did he die?]

Correcto:

I met the new technician. He **is** very personable.

Incorrecto:

We went to the new Italian restaurant on Vine last night. The atmosphere **was** wonderful. [What happened? Did it burn down during the night?]

Correcto:

We went to the new Italian restaurant on Vine last night. The atmosphere **is** wonderful.

Inclusive si un párrafo está escrito en el pasado, una declaración que continua siendo cierta es escrita en el tiempo presente.

Ejemplos:

During Galileo's time few people **believed** [past] that the earth **revolves** [present] around the sun.

The building engineer **explained** [past] to the plumber that the pipes **run** [present] parallel to the longest hallway in the building.

MODO SUBJUNTIVO

Cuando Tevya en *El violinista en el tejado* canta, "If I were a rich man…," él usa el verbo *were* para señalar que él, por cierto, no es un hombre rico. Normalmente, el verbo *was* sería usado con el sujeto *I,* pero *were* sirve un propósito especial. Esto se llama el subjuntivo *were.* Él indica una condición que es contraria a los hechos.

Ejemplos:

If I **were** a cat, I could sleep all day long and never have to worry about work.

If he **were** more attentive to details, he could be a copyeditor.

PRÁCTICA

En cada una de las siguientes oraciones encierre en un círculo la forma correcta del verbo.

11. Before I opened the door, I (ring, rang, had rung) the doorbell.

12. By the time I get to Phoenix, he will (read, have read) my goodbye letter.

13. The scientist explained why Saturn (is, was) surrounded by rings.

14. I would ask for a transfer if I (was, were) you.

15. The leaves on the trees have already (begin, began, begun) to fall.

16. The doctor took my pulse and (measures, measured) my blood pressure.

17. The president wishes he would (of, have) taken a stock option rather than a salary increase.

18. Boswick wishes he would have ordered a bigger sweatshirt because his (is, was) too small.

19. Ms. Grey announced that the floor manager (is, was) responsible for work schedules.

20. We could cut transportation costs if the plant (was, were) closer to the retail outlets.

RESPUESTAS

1. done	**6.** saw	**11.** had rung	**16.** measured
2. threw	**7.** begun	**12.** have read	**17.** have
3. spoke	**8.** gone	**13.** is	**18.** is
4. rung	**9.** bit	**14.** were	**19.** is
5. came	**10.** stolen	**15.** begun	**20.** were

Técnicas de aprendizaje

Escuche cuidadosamente a la gente. Escucha errores muy comunes como por ejemplo "I *could of gone* out if I had done my work"? Una vez que usted haga un hábito el escuchar errores en la conjugación de verbos, se dará cuenta de cuánta gente los comete. Algunos errores son tan aceptables que quizás no suenen tan extraños a un principio. Mientras más sensible sea usted a errores gramaticales, es menos probable que usted los vaya a hacer ya sea hablando o escribiendo.

USANDO VERBOS PARA ESCRIBIR EFECTIVAMENTE

RESUMEN DE LA LECCIÓN

Si los verbos dan significado, verbos motivadores realmente hacen que su escritura se acelere. Esta lección le mostrará como usar verbos para capturar el interes del lector.

Muy poca gente se molesta en leer algo que no es interesante. Incluso si lo leen, quizá no lleguen a entender el significado. Esta lección demuestra diferentes maneras de usar verbos para que su esctira sea llamativa e interesante para el lector. Lea los dos párrafos en la próxima página. ¿Cuál de ellos parece más llamativo e interesante? Ambos párrafos cuentan la misma historia, pero uno de ellos usa efectivamente los verbos para relatar la historia de tal manera que se la puede recordar más vivamente. Las oraciones son presentadas una a una, lado a lado, para que usted pueda compararlas más fácilmente.

Problema	Solución
When my brother was asked by the local Rotary Club to speak to them about computer programming, our entire family was amazed by the request.	When the local Rotary Club asked my brother to speak to them about computer programming, the request amazed our entire family.
A gasp was made by mother, a laugh was emitted by my father, and my head was shaken by me.	My mother gasped, my father laughed, and I just shook my head.
My brother is considered by us to be a shy, quiet computer nerd.	We consider my brother a shy, quiet computer nerd.
Since I am regarded by my family as the creative one, I was assigned by my brother the task of creating the visual aids.	Since everyone in the family regards me as the creative one, my brother assigned me the task of creating the visual aids.
The information was organized by my father.	My father organized the information.
Formal invitations were requested by my mother from the Rotary Club secretary and were sent by her to all of our friends.	My mother requested formal invitations from the Rotary Club secretary and sent them to all of our friends.
Organizing and rehearsing of the presentation was worked on by my family until 10:00 P.M. the night before the presentation.	Our family worked until 10:00 P.M. the night before the presentation, organizing and rehearsing.
The fact that he was ready was known by us.	We knew he was ready.
That night three feet of snow was dumped by the skies. The city was paralyzed, and all work and activities were canceled, including the Rotary Club meeting and my brother's presentation.	That night the skies dumped three feet of snow, paralyzing the city and causing all work and activities to be canceled, including the Rotary Club meeting and my brother's presentation.

VOZ ACTIVA VS. VOZ PASIVA

Cuando el sujeto de una oración ejecuta la acción del verbo, se dice que la oración es activa. Escriba usando verbos activos para hacer que su escritura sea más conversacional y más interesante. En una oración con un verbo activo, la persona o cosa que ejecuta la acción es llamada antes del verbo, o las palabras de acción, de una oración.

Esto puede sonar un tanto confuso, pero los ejemplos que siguen le ayudarán a ver la diferencia. Las palabras en itálicas demuestran quién está realizando la acción. Las palabras subrayadas son los verbos.

Verbos Pasivos	Verbos Activos
I <u>was taken</u> to my first horse show by my *grandfather*.	My *grandfather* <u>took</u> me to my first horse show.
I <u>was taught</u> to fish by my *mother* almost before I <u>was taught</u> to walk.	My *mother* <u>taught</u> me to fish almost before *I* <u>learned</u> to walk.

En cada una de las oraciones con verbos activos, la persona que realiza la acción es primeramente nombrada. Si usted observa todos estos ejemplos más cuidadosamente, se dará cuenta que las versiones con verbos activos son más cortas y claras. Estas oraciones suenan como conversaciones normales. Trate de lograr estos efectos en su escritura. La siguiente tabla demuestra las diferencias entre las voces activas y pasivas usando muchos de los tiempos verbales aprendidos en la Lección 10.

Tiempo Verbal	Active Voice	Pasive Voice
Presente	The *clerk* <u>opens</u> the mail.	The mail <u>is opened</u> by the *clerk*.
Pasado	The *clerk* <u>opened</u> the mail.	The mail <u>was opened</u> by the *clerk*.
Futuro	The *clerk* <u>will open</u> the mail.	The mail <u>will be opened</u> by the *clerk*.
Presente Perfecto	The *clerk* <u>has opened</u> the mail.	The mail <u>has been opened</u> by the *clerk*.
Pasado Perfecto	The *clerk* <u>had opened</u> the mail.	The mail <u>had been opened</u> by the *clerk*.
Futuro Perfecto	The *clerk* <u>will have opened</u> the mail.	The mail <u>will have been opened</u> by the *clerk*.

Muchos escritores prefieren la voz activa a la pasiva ya que ésta hace que la escritura sea más activa y más atrayente. Generalmente, los lectores encuentran que en la literatura la voz activa es más fácil de entender y de recordar. En ambas de las tablas anteriores, usted puede observar que las oraciones de voz activa son más cortas que las de la voz pasiva.

PRÁCTICA

En las siguientes oraciones, elija la oración que está escrita en voz activa. Las repuestas para cada grupo de preguntas se pueden encontrar al final de la lección.

1. a. Janice carefully packed the china.
   b. The china was carefully packed by Janice.

2. a. The CDs were purchased by my mother.
   b. My mother purchased the CDs.

3. a. Forty black candles were put on my mother's cake by Dad.

   b. Dad put forty black candles on my mother's cake.

4. a. The snow will be cleared by the plow.

   b. The plow will clear the snow.

5. a. Citizens believe that judges do not hand out adequate penalties for drug dealers.

   b. It is believed by the citizens that adequate penalties for drug dealers are not being handed
   out by judges.

6. a. Coins are often thrown in fountains by tourists.

   b. Tourists often throw coins in fountains.

7. a. Every Sunday morning millions of children watch TV.

   b. Every Sunday morning TV is being watched by millions of children.

CUANDO SE PUEDE USAR LA VOZ PASIVA

Además de no tener carácter propio, la voz pasiva también puede indicar el deseo de no tomar ninguna responsabilidad por las acciones o la intención de no alentar preguntas. La oración que sigue demuestra este caso.

It has been recommended that twenty workers be laid off within the next three months.

A parte de no tener vida, la voz pasiva también señala las ganas de no tomar responsabilidad por acciones o intenciones para no alentar preguntas. Muchas veces los dictadores tienden a escribir y a hablar usando la voz pasiva. Una persona pensativa va a ver más allá de la voz pasiva. ¿Quién está recomendando la acción? ¿Por qué? ¿Quién va a mentir? ¿Cómo serán elegidos los trabajadores?

De todas maneras, la voz pasiva no es siempre mala. A veces, pero muy raramente, ésta funciona mucho mejor que la voz activa. Las situaciones en la que se prefiere la voz pasiva son indicadas a continuación.

1. **Cuando el objeto es más importante que el agente de la acción (el actante).**

A veces, en la literatura científica, el objeto y no el actante es el centro o el foco de la oración. El siguiente párrafo ha sido escrito en ambas voces; pasiva y activa respectivamente. El primer párrafo es más apropiado en esta ocasión debido a que la operación y no el doctor es el centro de la acción. El párrafo no puede ser escrito en voz activa sin tener que dar importancia al actante, el doctor. Por consiguiente, la voz pasiva es la mejor elección en este caso.

Voz Pasiva

The three-inch incision is made right above the pubic bone. Plastic clips are used to clamp off blood vessels and minimize bleeding. The skin is folded back and secured with clamps. Next, the stomach muscle is cut at a fifteen-degree angle, right top to bottom left.

Voz Activa

The doctor makes a three-inch incision right above the pubic bone. He uses plastic clips to clamp off the blood vessels and minimize bleeding. He folds back the skin and secures it with clamps. Next, he cuts the stomach muscle at a fifteen-degree angle, right top to bottom left.

2. Cuando el agente de la acción (actante) es desconocido o secreto.

A veces un reportero protejerá una fuente de información por escrito, "It was reported that...." En otras instancias, quizás a veces, nadie sabe quien cometió la acción: "First State Bank was robbed...."

3. Cuando la voz pasiva resulta en oraciones cortas sin alejarse del significado.

Generalmente, la voz activa es más corta y más concisa que la voz pasiva. Pero hay muchas excepciones. Examine los ejemplos en la tabla que sigue. Si usando la voz pasiva le ayuda a salvar tiempo y problemas ademas de resultar en oraciones más cortas, úsela.

Activa	Pasiva
The designers of the study told the interviewer to give interviewees an electric shock each time they smiled.	The interviewer was told to give the interviewees an electric shock each time they smiled.
The police apprehended Axtell, the detectives interrogated him, and the grand jury indicted him.	Axtell was apprehended, interrogated, and indicted.

OTRAS CONSTRUCCIONES VERBALES COMPLICADAS

Si el pensamiento es un tren, entonces los verbos son las ruedas que mueven la carga de un lugar a otro. El pensamiento se va a mover más rápido si es transportado por muchas ruedas grandes y fuertes. Las siguientes son algunas de las construcciones que tiene que evadir y muestran cómo puede elegir verbos mejores y más significativos.

USO DE VERBOS SER Y ESTAR

Estos verbos tienen la forma del verbo ser (to be): *am, is, are, was, were,* etc. Estos verbos no actuan tan dinámicamente como los verbos de acción. Siguiendo la analogía anterior, donde el pensamiento es como un tren, estos verbos son ruedas muy pequeñas, incapaz de mover rápida y fácilmente ideas mucho más grandes. Si usted sólo tiene que decir cosas sin importancia, use estos verbos. Si sus ideas son más complejas e interesantes, éstas van a requerir verbos más complejos y mucho mejores.

Vea el párrafo de la página que sigue. En la primera versión los verbos son ser o estar. En la segunda versión, verbos activos hacen que el párrafo sea más interesante.

Verbos Ser y Estar

The class was outside during noon recess. The sunshine was bright. Earlier in the day there was rain, but later the weather was pleasant. The breeze was slight; the newly fallen leaves were in motion. Across the street from the school was an ice cream truck. It was what the children were looking at longingly.

Verbos de Acción

The class played outside during noon recess. The sun shone brightly. Earlier in the day, rain had fallen, but later pleasant weather arrived. A slight breeze blew the newly fallen leaves. The children looked longingly at the ice cream truck across the street.

CONVIRTIENDO VERBOS EN NOMBRES

Naturalmente, si usted saca las ruedas del tren del pensamiento y las pone en una superficie plana de cargo, el tren no se va a mover como lo hacía anteriormente. Observe las dos oraciones que siguen. En la primera, muchos verbos han sido transformados en nombres para que la pieza escrita suene "intelectual." En lugar de eso, esta "verb-ificación" hace que la selección sea inclusive más difícil de leer. La segunda oración coumunica la misma información con el mismo nivel de sofisticación, al convertir los nombres nuevamente en verbos la lectura es más fácil. Las formas verbales han sido marcadas para que puedan ser identificadas más fácilmente.

The customer service division **is** now conducting an assessment of its system for the reaction to consumer concerns and the development of new products.

The customer service division **is assessing** its system for **reacting** to consumer concerns and **developing** new products.

AÑADIENDO VERBOS AUXILIARES INNECESARIOS

Generalmente, si usted no necesita un verbo auxiliar (*have, had, is, are, was, were, will, would,* y demás) para añadir significado (vea Lección 10), no use ninguno.

Verbos Auxiliares Innecesarios	Versión Corregida
After lunch we *would meet* in the lounge.	After lunch we *met* in the lounge.
The temperature *was rising* steadily.	The temperature *rose* steadily.
Every morning the doors *will open* at 8:00.	Every morning the doors *open* at 8:00.

COMENZANDO CON *THERE* O CON *IT*

Muchas oraciones no necesariamente comienzan con *there is/are/was/were* o con *it is/was.* Usualmente lo que esas palabras hacen es posponer el comienzo del pensamiento. Las oraciones en la próxima página demuestran como estas palabras absorventes pueden ser eliminadas de lo que usted escribe.

There o *It* Innecesarios	Versión Corregida
There are three people who are authorized to use this machinery.	Three people are authorized to use this machinery.
There is one good way to handle this problem: to ignore it.	One good way to handle this problem is to ignore it.
It was a perfect evening for a rocket launch.	The evening was perfect for a rocket launch.
There were several people standing in line waiting for the bus.	Several people stood in line waiting for the bus.

USO DE VERBOS INTERESANTES Y MOTIVADORES

Si usted quiere mover sus ideas eficientemente, tenga en cuenta la precisión y busque verbos que creen una imagen en la mente del lector. Compare las siguientes oraciones para ver estos principios en acción.

Sin Motivación	Muy Motivado
At my barbershop, someone does your nails and your shoes while your hair is being cut.	At my barbershop, someone manicures your nails and shines your shoes as your hair is cut.
Violent cartoons are harmful to children's emotional development and sense of reality.	Violent cartoons stunt children's emotional development and distort their sense of reality.

PRÁCTICA

Elija la mejor oración del siguiente grupo. Tenga en mente todo lo que usted ha aprendido en esta lección.

8. a. Much concern is being voiced by the citizens over the failure to balance the budget.
   b. Citizens are voicing much concern over the failure to balance the budget.

9. a. The game was played by three old men and a young boy.
   b. Three old men and a young boy played the game.

10. a. Those who evaluate law enforcement officers consider procedures that avoid lawsuits more valuable than those that effectively enforce the laws.
   b. Those responsible for the evaluation of law enforcement officers have a greater consideration for the discharge of procedures that will result in the avoidance of lawsuits than those resulting in effective enforcement of the laws.

11. a. There are many reasons that you should avoid foods that are high in fat.
   b. You should avoid high fat foods for many reasons.

12. a. After dinner every night we would make popcorn.
   b. We made popcorn every night after dinner.

13. a. We gobbled up donuts every morning before work.
   b. We had donuts every morning before work.

14. a. A computer technician must have solid people skills.
   b. It is necessary for a computer technician to have solid people skills.

Técnicas de aprendizaje

Hoy, mientras usted lee un periódico, una revista, libros u otros materiales busque ejemplos de oraciones que emplean la voz activa y pasiva. Trate de convertir algunas de las oraciones en voz pasiva a voz activa y viceversa. ¿Cuál versión es más efectiva?

RESPUESTAS

1. a.	**5.** a.	**9.** b.	**13.** a.
2. b.	**6.** b.	**10.** a.	**14.** a.
3. b.	**7.** a.	**11.** b.	
4. b.	**8.** b.	**12.** b.	

CONCORDANCIA ENTRE SUJETO Y VERBO

RESUMEN DE LA LECCIÓN

Generalmente, y sin pensarlo, cuando usted habla o escribe se asegura de que sus sujetos y verbos concuerdan. Son muy pocas situaciones que causan dificultad cuando se refiere a la concordancia entre sujeto y verbo. Esta lección le mostrará cómo solucionar esos cuantos problemas de escritura.

C uando el sujeto de una cláusula—la persona o cosa ejecutando la acción—concuerda en número con el verbo, se dice que el sujeto y el verbo *agree*. La mayor parte de la gente nativa de habla inglesa no tiene ningún problema con esto. Unas pocas construcciones gramaticales poseen la mayor parte de estos problemas. Esta lección explica el concepto de la concordancia entre sujeto y verbo, además le provee con problemas prácticos para ayudarle.

CONCORDANCIA ENTRE NOMBRES SUJETOS Y VERBOS

En el lenguaje escrito, un sujeto tiene que concordar en número con su verbo. En otras palabras, si el sujeto es singular, el verbo tiene que ser singular. Si el sujeto es plural, el verbo tiene que ser plural. Si no está seguro de que un verbo sea plural o singular, tome esta simple prueba. En las siguientes oraciones, llene los espacios con la verdadera conjugación del verbo. La mejor forma verbal que completa la primera oración es singular. La mejor forma verbal que completa la segunda oración es plural.

Singular	**Plural**
One person _____.	Two people _____.

Observe estos ejemplos usando los verbos *speak, do* y *was*. Trate de hacerlo por usted mismo usando cualquier verbo que lo confunda. Contrariamente de los nombres, verbos que terminan en *s* son generalmente singulares.

Singular	Plural
One person <u>speaks</u>.	Two people <u>speak</u>.
One person <u>does</u>.	Two people <u>do</u>.
One person <u>was</u>.	Two people <u>were</u>.

PROBLEMAS ESPECIALES
Doesn't/Don't y Wasn't/Weren't

Algunas personas tienen problemas con *doesn't/don't* (contracciones de *does not* y de *do not*) y con *wasn't/weren't* (contracciones de *was not* y de *were not*). *Doesn't* y *wasn't* son singulares; *don't* y *weren't* son plurales. Si usted dice toda la frase en lugar de la contracción, tenga por seguro que estará usando la forma correcta.

Frases que siguen al sujeto

Tenga cuidado especial con el sujeto de una oración. No se deje llevar por una frase que sigue a éste y que le haga usar un verbo que no concuerda con el mismo. En los siguientes ejemplos, los sujetos y verbos están marcados.

> **One** of the print orders **is** missing.
> The software **designs** by Liu Chen **are** complex and colorful.
> A **handbook** with thorough instructions **comes** with this product.
> The **president**, along with her three executive assistants, **leaves** for the conference tomorrow.

Sujetos singulares especiales

Algunos nombres son singulares pese a que terminan en *s*. Pese a su forma plural, los mismos requieren un verbo singular porque uno tiene que pensar en ellos como una cosa singular. La mayor parte de los nombres de la lista que sigue son singulares. Algunos pueden ser o singular o plural, dependiendo de su uso en la oración.

measles	physics	sports
mumps	economics	politics
news	mathematics	statistics
checkers	civics	
marbles (the game)	athletics	

Estos son algunos ejemplos para mostrar cómo estas palabras funcionan en oraciones.

The **news is** on at 6:00.

Checkers is my favorite game.

Sports is a healthy way to reduce stress.

Low-impact **sports are** recommended for older adults.

Palabras que declaran una cantidad singular o el tiempo requieren el uso del verbo en el singular. Examine cuidadosamente una oración para ver si la cantidad o el tiempo es considerado una medida singular.

Two dollars **is** the price of that small replacement part. [single amount]

Two dollars **are** lying on my dresser.

Three hours **was** required to complete this simulation. [single measure]

Three hours of each day **were** spent rehearsing.

Three-quarters of her time **is** spent writing.

PRÁCTICA

En las siguientes oraciones, encierre el verbo correcto en un círculo. Las respuestas para cada una de las preguntas pueden ser encontradas al final de la lección.

1. When the comedian (jokes, joke), the audience members (laughs, laugh).

2. A single flower now (grows, grow) where the trees used to (grows, grow).

3. Manuel (speaks, speak) English, but his parents (speaks, speak) Spanish.

4. The clerk (rings, ring) up the sales while the customers (waits, wait) in line.

5. The sopranos (hums, hum) softly while the tenor soloist (sings, sing)

6. The new colors (doesn't, don't) look especially appealing.

7. The door to the building (wasn't, weren't) locked last night.

8. The drive-up teller line (doesn't, don't) open until 9:30 on Saturday mornings.

9. Marge didn't receive the message because the phones (wasn't, weren't) working.

10. He (doesn't, don't) remember if the ties (is, are) still on sale.

11. One of the clerks (is, are) sorting the rack of trousers that (was, were) mislabeled.

12. The petty cash box, along with the ticket receipts, (is, are) turned in at the end of the day.

13. These statistics (is, are) the result of a flawed study.

14. Statistics (was, were) my most difficult math course in high school.

15. Half of the bagel (was, were) eaten.

16. Half of the bagels (was, were) eaten.

CONCORDANCIA ENTRE PRONOMBRES SUJETOS Y VERBOS

Pronombres sujetos presentan un problema inclusive para las personas de habla inglés más sofisticadas. Algunos pronombres son siempre singulares; otros siempre son plurales. Una gran parte de estos puede ser singular o plural.

PRONOMBRES SINGULARES

Estos pronombres son siempre singulares.

each	anybody	everyone	one
either	anyone	no one	somebody
neither	everybody	nobody	someone

Los pronombres de la primera columna son aquellos que con mucha frequencia se usan equivocadamente. Usted puede evadir problemas al añadir mentalmente la palabra *one* después del pronombre y omitir las otras palabras entre el pronombre y el verbo. Vea los siguientes ejemplos para ver como se ejecuta esto.

Each of the men wants his own car.
Each *one* wants his own car.
Either of the salesclerks knows where the sale merchandise is located.
Either *one* knows where the sale merchandise is located.

Estas oraciones pueden sonar un tanto extrañas ya que mucha gente usa incorrectamente estos pronombres, y seguramente usted se ha acostumbrado a oírlos de esa manera. Pese a eso, el truco de la substitución (*one* por las palabras que siguen al pronombre) le ayudará a solucionar este problema.

CUIDADO CON LAS PREGUNTAS

Con preguntas que comienzan con *has* o *have*, recuerde que *has* es singular mientras que *have* es plural. En una pregunta, ponga atención especial a la combinación de verbo y sujeto. A propósito, el verbo correcto es más fácil de identificar si usted transforma la pregunta en una declaración afirmativa.

Forma Interrogativa	Forma Afirmativa
(Is, Are) some of the customers noticing the difference?	Some of the customers **are** noticing the difference.
(Has, Have) either of the shipments arrived?	Either [*one*] of the shipments **has** arrived.
(Does, Do) each of the terminals have a printer?	Each [*one*] of the terminals **does** have a printer.

PRONOMBRES PLURALES

Estos pronombres son siempre plurales y requieren un verbo plural.

both	many
few	several

PRONOMBRES SINGULARES/PLURALES

Los siguientes pronombres pueden ser singulares o plurales. Las palabras o frases preposicionales que las siguen, determinan si éstas son singulares o plurales. Si la frase que sigue al pronombre contiene un nombre o pronombre plural, el verbo tiene que ser plural. Si la frase que sigue al pronombre contiene un nombre o pronombre singular, el verbo tiene que ser singular. Vea como se hace esto en las oraciones que siguen a la lista de pronombres. Las palabras claves han sido marcadas.

all	none
any	some
most	

Singular	Plural
All of the **work is** finished.	**All** of the **jobs are** finished.
Is any of the **pizza** left?	**Are** any of the **pieces** of pizza left?
Most of the **grass has** turned brown.	**Most** of the **blades** of grass **have** turned brown.
None of the **time was** wasted.	**None** of the **minutes were** wasted.
Some of the **fruit was** spoiled.	**Some** of the **apples were** spoiled.

PRÁCTICA

En cada una de las siguientes oraciones encierre en un círculo la forma correcta del verbo. Las respuestas están al final de la lección.

17. Neither of these keys (unlocks, unlock) the back door.

18. Each of the community profiles (takes, take) a creative approach to advertising.

19. All of the tasks (has, have) been assigned.

20. Some of the residents (was, were) pleased with the new development.

21. Either of these light fixtures (is, are) suitable for my office.

22. (Was, Were) any of the samples defective?

23. (Do, Does) each of the phones have multiple lines?

24. (Has, Have) either of the partners announced an intention to reorganize?

25. Neither of our largest accounts (needs, need) to be serviced at this time.

26. Both of the applicants (seems, seem) qualified.

27. A woman in one of my classes (works, work) at the Civic Center box office.

28. None of our resources (goes, go) to outside consultants.

29. A good knowledge of the rules (helps, help) you understand the game.

30. Each of these prescriptions (causes, cause) bloating and irritability.

31. (Have, Has) either of them ever arrived on time?

ESTRUCTURAS ESPECIALES EN ORACIONES

SUJETOS COMPUESTOS

- Si dos nombres o pronombres están unidos por *and*, éstos requieren un verbo en plural.

    He and she **want** to buy a new house.

    Jack and Jill **want** to buy a new house.

- Si dos nombres o pronombres están unidos por *or* o *nor*, estos requieren un verbo en singular. Piense en ellos como en dos oraciones separadas y nunca se equivocará en su conjugación.

    Jack or Jill **wants** to buy a new house.

    Jack **wants** to buy a new house.

    Jill **wants** to buy a new house.

- Sujetos singulares o plurales unidos por *or* o *nor* requieren un verbo que concuerde con el sujeto más cercano al verbo.

    Neither management nor the **employees like** the new agreement.

    Neither the employees nor the **management likes** the new agreement.

ASEGÚRESE DE ENCONTRAR AL SUJETO

Verbos tienen que concordar con el sujeto y no con el complemento de una oración. El verbo, una forma de *be*, une al sujeto y al complemento, pero usualmente primero se escribe el sujeto y el complemento viene después del verbo.

> **Taxes were** the main challenge facing the financial department.
>
> The main **challenge** facing the financial department **was** taxes.
>
> A serious **problem** for most automobile commuters **is** traffic jams.
>
> **Traffic jams are** a serious problem for most automobile commuters.

Preguntas y oraciones que comienzan con *There* o *Here*

Cuando una oración es interrogativa o comienza con palabras como *there* o *here*, el sujeto sigue el verbo. Localice el sujeto de la oración y asegúrese que el verbo esté de acuero con el mismo. En los ejemplos que siguen, los sujetos y verbos están marcados en la forma correcta de las oraciones.

Incorrecto	Correcto
What is the conditions of the contract?	What **are** the **conditions** of the contract?
Why is her reports always so disorganized?	Why **are** her **reports** always so disorganized?
Here's the records you requested.	Here **are** the **records** you requested.
There is four people seeking this promotion.	There **are** four **people** seeking this promotion.

Oraciones Invertidas

Oraciones invertidas también contienen sujetos que siguen, en vez de preceder, los verbos. Encuentre el sujeto de la oración y asegúrese de que el verbo está de acuerdo con éste. En los ejemplos de oraciones que siguen, los sujetos y los verbos de las oraciones correctas han sido marcados.

Incorrecto	Correcto
Beside the front desk stands three new vending machines.	Beside the front desk **stand** three new vending **machines**.
Suddenly, out of the thicket comes three large bucks.	Suddenly, out of the thicket **come** three large **bucks**.
Along with our highest recommendation goes our best wishes in your new job.	Along with our highest recommendation **go** our best **wishes** in your new job.

PRÁCTICA

En cada una de las siguientes oraciones encierre en un círculo la forma correcta del verbo. Las respuestas están al final de la lección.

32. Every other day either Bert or Ernie (takes, take) out the trash.

33. Neither the style nor the color (matches, match) what we currently have.

34. Either the associates or the manager (orders, order) the merchandise.

35. Either the manager or the associates (orders, order) the merchandise.

36. (Is, Are) the men's wear or the women's wear department on the ground floor?

37. Mr. Jefson's passion (is, are) economics.

38. (Was, Were) there any furniture sets left over after the sale?

39. There (isn't, aren't) many days left before the Grand Opening.

40. Here (is, are) the information you requested.

41. Off into the horizon (runs, run) the herd of buffalo.

Técnicas de aprendizaje

Escuche a la gente mientras habla. ¿Usa los verbos correctamente? ¿Usa la forma correcta del tiempo verbal? ¿Hay concordancia entre los sujetos y verbos? Probablemente no es una buena idea corregir a miembros de su familia, amigos, y compañeros de trabajo, pero usted puede practicar al escuchar los errores que ellos puedan cometer al hablar.

RESPUESTAS

1. jokes, laugh
2. grows, grow
3. speaks, speak
4. rings, wait
5. hum, sings
6. don't
7. wasn't
8. doesn't
9. weren't
10. doesn't, are
11. is, was
12. is
13. are
14. was
15. was
16. were
17. unlocks
18. takes
19. have
20. were
21. is
22. Were
23. Does
24. Has
25. needs
26. seem
27. works
28. go
29. helps
30. causes
31. Has
32. takes
33. matches
34. orders
35. order
36. Is
37. is
38. Were
39. aren't
40. is
41. runs

L·E·C·C·I·Ó·N

USO DE PRONOMBRES

RESUMEN DE LA LECCIÓN

Con mucha frecuencia, los pronombres son tan mal usados en las conversaciones que mucha gente no sabe como evitarlos cuando escribe. Esta lección le mostrará como evitar los errores más comunes en el uso de pronombres.

Un pronombre es una palabra que se usa en lugar de un nombre. Pronombres mal usados son notables y difieren del mensaje de algo escrito. Esta lección explica los principios básicos del uso de los pronombres y delinea los problemas más comunes: concordancia, caso, pares de nombres y pronombres, construcciones incompletas, referencias ambiguas de pronombres, y pronombres reflexivos.

PRONOMBRES Y ANTECEDENTES

El nombre representado por un pronombre es llamado *antecedente*. El prefijo *ante* significa que viene antes. Generalmente, en una oración, el antecedente está escrito antes del pronombre. En las siguientes oraciones, los pronombres han sido escritos en itálicas y los antecedentes (las palabras que éstos representan) han sido subrayados.

The government <u>workers</u> received *their* paychecks.

Jane thought *she* saw the missing boy and reported *him* to the police.

The shift supervisor hates these accidents because *he* thinks *they* can be easily avoided.

Un pronombre debe igualar el número de sus antecedentes. En otras palabras, si el antecedente es singular, el pronombre debe ser singular. Si el antecedente es plural, el pronombre debe ser plural. Muy poca gente comete errores **apareando** un pronombre con un nombre antecedente. De todas maneras, a veces un pronombre es el antecedente para otro pronombre. En la Lección 12 usted aprendió sobre los pronombres singulares. Ésta es la lista.

each	anybody	everyone	one
either	anyone	no one	somebody
neither	everybody	nobody	someone

- Un pronombre con una de las palabras de esta lista como su antecedente tiene que ser singular.

  Each (singular) of the men brought *his* (singular) favorite tool to the bachelor party.

  Everyone (singular) who wants to be in the "Toughman" contest should pay up *his* (singular) life insurance.

  Somebody left *her* purse underneath the desk.

  Neither of the occupants could locate *his* (or *her*) key to the apartment.

- Si dos o más nombres o pronombres singulares están unidos por *and,* use la forma plural.

  Buddha and Muhammad built religions around *their* philosophies.

  If he and she want to know where I was, *they* should ask me.

- Si dos o más nombres o pronombres singulares están unidos por *or,* use un pronombre singular.

  Matthew or Jacob will loan you *his* calculator.

  The elephant or the moose will furiously protect *its* young.

- Si un nombre y pronombre singular y plural están unidos por *or,* el pronombre concuerda con el pronombre o nombre que representa y que está más cercano.

  Neither the soldiers nor the sergeant was sure of *his* location.

  Neither the sergeant nor the soldiers were sure of *their* location.

PRÁCTICA

En cada una de las siguientes oraciones, marque en un círculo la forma correcta del pronombre. Las respuestas están al final del capítulo.

1. No one in (her, their) right mind would agree to drive that contraption.

2. Neither the students nor the teacher brought (his, their) book to class.

3. Anyone who wants a ticket to the banquet should sign (his, their) name on this sheet.

4. Ask someone in this office where the instruction manual is, and (he, they) probably can't tell you.

5. Neither Alexis nor Heidi will inconvenience (herself, themselves) to cover your mistake.

6. If you break a print head or a roller on the printer, (it, they) is hard to replace.

7. I know of someone who might give you (her, their) notes from the course.

8. Almost anybody can improve (his, their) writing by using this book.

9. If you want to make a good impression on a customer, don't talk down to (her, them).

CASOS DE PRONOMBRES

La mayor parte de la gente no tiene problemas en el uso del *I* o del *me*, o cuando usa *my*. Estos tres pronombres demuestran los tres casos para la primera persona del singular: nominativo (*I*), objetivo (*me*), y posesivo (*my*). La tabla que sigue, muestra los casos de todos los pronombres, tanto en singular como en plural.

CASOS DE PRONOMBRES PERSONALES		
Nominativo	**Objetivo**	**Posesivo**
I	me	my
we	us	our
you	you	your
he	him	his
she	her	her
they	them	their
it	it	its

Casos de pronombres **nominativos** (aquellos de la primera columna), son usados como sujetos o complementos siguiendo a los verbos unificadores (*am, is, are, was, were*)—cualquier forma del verbo *to be*. Casos de pronombres nominativos que siguen al verbo pueden parecerle extraños porque muy poca gente los usa correctamente.

> **They** left a few minutes early in order to mail the package. [sujeto]
> **I** looked all over town for the type of paper you wanted. [sujeto]
> The doctor who removed my appendix was **he**. [sigue a un verbo conector]
> "This is **she**, or it is **I**," said Barbara into the phone. [sigue a un verbo conector]
> The winners of the sales contest were **he** and **she**. [sigue a un verbo conector]

Casos de pronombres **objetivos** (aquellos de la columna del centro) son usados como objetos que siguen un verbo activo o como objetos de una preposición.

> The help line representative gave **him** an answer over the phone. [sigue a un verbo activo]
> Of all these samples, I prefer **them**. [sigue a un verbo activo]
> We went to lunch with Sammy and **him**. [objeto de la preposición *with*]
> We couldn't tell whether the package was for **them** or **us**. [objeto(s) de la preposición *for*]

Casos de pronombres **posesivos** (aquellos de la tercera columna) demuestran pertenencia. Muy pocos anglo-parlantes hacen mal uso de los pronombres posesivos. La mayor parte de los problemas de pronombres ocurren con los casos del nominativo y del objetivo.

PROBLEMAS CON EL CASO DEL PRONOMBRE

Un solo pronombre en una oración es fácil de usarlo correctamente. Por cierto, mucha gente de habla inglesa podría identificar los errores en las siguientes oraciones.

> **Me** worked on the project with **he**.
> My neighbor gave **she** a ride to work.

Mucha gente sabe que **Me** en la primera oración, debería ser **I**, y que **he** debería ser **him**. Ellos también se darían cuenta de que **she** en la segunda oración debe ser **her**. Esta clase de error es fácil de identificar cuándo los pronombres son usados individualmente en una oración. El problema ocurre cuando un pronombre es usado con un nombre o con otro pronombre. Vea si puede identificar los errores en las siguientes oraciones.

Incorrecto:
> The grand marshall rode with Shane and I.
> Donna and me are going to the Civic Center.
> The stage manager spoke to my brother and I.

Los errores en estas oraciones son más difíciles de identificar que en aquellas oraciones con un sólo pronombre. Si usted convierte la oración que contiene dos pronombres en dos oraciones separadas, el error se puede ver claramente.

Correcto:
> The grand marshall rode with Shane.
> The grand marshall rode with **me** (no *I*).
> Donna is going to the Civic Center. [Use el verbo singular *is* en lugar de *are*.]
> **I** (no *me*) am going to the Civic Center. [Use el verbo *am* en lugar de *are*.]
> The stage manager spoke to my brother.
> The stage manager spoke to **me** (no *I*).

El dividir una oración en dos no funciona muy bién con la preposición *between*. Si usted substituye *with* por *between*, entonces el error es más fácil de reconocer.

> The problem is between (she, her) and (I, me).
> The problem is with **her**. (not *she*)
> The problem is with **me**. (not *I*)

PRÁCTICA

En las siguientes oraciones encierre en un círculo los pronombres correctos. Las respuestas están al final de la lección.

10. Andy or Arvin will bring (his, their) camera so (he, they) can take pictures of the party.

11. Benny and (he, him) went to the movies with Bonnie and (I, me).

12. Neither my cousins nor my uncle knows what (he, they) will do tomorrow.

13. Why must it always be (I, me) who cleans up the lounge?

14. The pilot let (he, him) and (I, me) look at the instrument panel.

15. Have you heard the latest news about (she, her) and (they, them)?

16. My friend and (I, me) both want to move to another location.

PARES QUE NO CONSTITUYEN PRONOMBRES

A veces en una oración, un nombre es inmediatamente seguido por un pronombre. Para asegurarse que usted está usando el pronombre correcto, omita el nombre de este par. Estudie los siguientes ejemplos para ver cómo se implementa esto.

PRONOMBRES EN PARES QUE NO CONSTITUYEN PRONOMBRES	
¿Qué Pronombre?	**Remueva el Nombre**
(We, Us) support personnel wish to lodge a complaint.	**We** wish to lodge a complaint.
They gave the job to (we, us) inventory staffers.	They gave the job to **us**.
The committee threw (we, us) retirees a huge end-of-the-year party.	The committee threw **us** a huge end-of-the-year party.

CONSTRUCCIONES INCOMPLETAS

A veces un pronombre está al final de una oración y sigue una palabra comparativa como *than* o *as*.

> Harold spent as much time on this project as (they, them).
> Duane can build cabinets better than (I, me).
> The long day exhausted us more than (they, them).
> My youngest child is now taller than (I, me).

En cada una de estas oraciones parte del significado está implícito. Para determinar qué pronombre es correcto, complete la oración mentalmente y use el pronombre que tenga más sentido.

> Harold spent as much time on this project as *they did*.
> Harold spent as much time on this project as *he spent on them*.

La primera oración tiene más sentido, entonces *they* no sería la respuesta correcta.

> Duane can build cabinets better than *I can*.
> Duane can build cabinets better than *he can build me*.

La primera oración tiene más sentido, entonces *I* es el pronombre correcto.

> The long day exhausted us more than *they did*.
> The long day exhausted us more than *it did them*.

La segunda oración tiene más sentido, entonces *them* es la opción correcta.

> My youngest child is now taller than *I am*.

No hay ninguna posibilidad de completar la oración usando el pronombre *me,* entonces *I* es la opción correcta.

La selección de un pronombre es de importancia vital si es que la oración tiene sentido de cualquier modo. La siguiente oración puede ser completada usando ambos pronombres, cualquiera de los dos tiene sentido. La selección de pronombres controla el significado. El escritor tiene que ser muy cuidadoso en elegir el pronombre correcto si es que se quiere que el significado sea descrito exactamente.

> I work with Assad more than (she, her).
> I work with Assad more than *she does*.
> I work with Assad more than *I work with her*.

Use el pronombre que refleja el propósito del significado.

PRONOMBRES Y SUS REFERENCIAS AMBIGUAS

A veces, una oración es escrita de tal manera que un pronombre puede referirse a uno o más antecedentes. Cuando esto pasa, se dice que el significado es *ambiguo*. En los siguientes ejemplos, los pronombres ambiguos han sido puestos en itálicas, y los posibles antecedentes han sido subrayados.

> When Eric spoke to his girlfriend's father, *he* was very polite.
> Remove the door from the frame and paint *it*.
> Jamie told Linda *she* should be ready to go within an hour.
> Pat told Craig *he* had been granted an interview.

Vea cómo las oraciones a continuación han sido escritas nuevamente para clarificar sus referencias ambiguas.

> Eric was very polite when he spoke to his girlfriend's father.
> Paint the door after removing it from the frame.
> Jamie told Linda to be ready to go within an hour.
> Pat told Craig that Craig had been granted an interview.

PRONOMBRES REFLEXIVOS IMPROPIOS

Un pronombre reflexivo es uno que incluye la palabra *self* o *selves: myself, yourself, himself, herself, ourself, themselves*. La siguiente sección explica maneras en las cuales pronombres reflexivos son a menudo mal usados.

- Los pronombres posesivos *his* y *their* no pueden convertirse en reflexivos.
  Incorrecto:
  > They decided to do the remodeling theirselves.
  > Mark wanted to arrange the meeting hisself.

  Correcto:
  > They decided to do the remodeling *themselves*.
  > Mark wanted to arrange the meeting *himself*.

- Evite el uso de un pronombre reflexivo cuando un pronombre personal funciona en una oración.
  Incorrecto:
  > Three associates and myself chose the architect for the building.
  > The preliminary results of the poll were revealed only to ourselves.

  Correcto:
  > Three associates and *I* chose the architect for the building.
  > The preliminary results of the poll were revealed only to *us*.

Técnicas de aprendizaje

Identifique uno o dos de los errores que usted comete cuando usa pronombres. En su conversación, haga un esfuerzo conciente de usar los pronombres correctamente por lo menos tres veces.

RESPUESTAS

1. her	**5.** herself	**9.** her	**13.** I
2. his	**6.** it	**10.** his, he	**14.** him, me
3. his	**7.** her	**11.** he, me	**15.** her, them
4. he	**8.** his	**12.** he	**16.** I

VERBOS Y PRONOMBRES PROBLEMÁTICOS

14

RESUMEN DE LA LECCIÓN

¿*Sit* o *set*? ¿*Your* o *you're*? ¿*There* o *their*? O es que es ¿*they're*? Saber cómo usar estos tipos de problemas es una señal de ser un escritor educado. Esta lección le enseñará cómo.

E sta lección cubre verbos problemáticos como *lie/lay, sit/set, rise/raise,* y sus varias formas. La lección también cubre los pronombres problemáticos como *its/it's, your/you're, whose/who's, who/that/which,* y *there/they're/their*. Usted puede ser distinguido como un buén escritor si usted es capáz dc usar estos verbos y pronombres correctamente en situaciones formales de escritura.

VERBOS PROBLEMATICOS

LIE/LAY

Muy poca gente usa correctamente *lie* y *lay* y sus partes principales, quizás se deba a que muy pocas personas saben la diferencia entre el significado de ambas. El verbo *lie* significa *to rest or recline*. El verbo *lay* significa *to put or place*. La tabla en la página que sigue muestra las partes principales de cada uno de estos verbos. Sus significados, escritos en la forma correcta, aparecen en paréntesis.

FORMAS DE *LIE* Y *LAY*

Presente	Progresivo	Pasado	Pasado Participio*
lie, lies	lying	lay	lain
(rest, rests)	(resting)	(rested)	(rested)
lay, lays	laying	laid	laid
(place, places)	(placing)	(placed)	(placed)

El participio pasado es la forma usada conjuntamente con have, has *o* had.

Para usar la forma correcta de *lie* o *lay,* simplemente observe el significado entre paréntesis. Elija la palabra en paréntesis que tiene más sentido y use la forma correspondiente de *lie* o *lay.* A veces, ninguna de las palabras parece específicamente apropiada. De todas maneras, elija la opción que, entre todas, tenga más sentido. Si la oración contiene la palabra *down,* mentalmente borre la palabra de la oración para hacer que el verbo apropiado sea más obvio. Examine estos ejemplos para ver como se hace.

The garbage cans are _____ in the middle of the street. [Requiere progresivo]
Resting tiene mejor sentido que *placing.*
Elija *lying.*

Keith told Nan to _____ the mail on the dining room table. [Requires presente]
Place tiene mejor sentido que *rest.*
Choose *lay.*

The sandwiches _____ in the sun for over an hour before we ate them. [Requires past]
Rested makes better sense than *placed.*
Elija *lay.*

Yesterday afternoon, I _____ down for an hour. [Requiere pasado]
Remueva la palabra *down.*
Rested tiene mejor sentido que *placed.*
Elija *lay.*

Barry thought he had _____ the papers near the copy machine. [Requiere participio pasado]
Placed tiene mejor sentido que *rested.*
Elija *laid.*

PRÁCTICA

En cada uno de los espacios en blanco, escriba la forma correcta de *lie* o *lay*. Las respuestas pueden ser encontradas al final de la lección.

1. After the alarm sounded, I _____ in bed for another hour.

2. _____ the packages on the mailroom floor.

3. The latest edition of the newspaper _____ on the desk.

4. The paper carrier _____ the latest edition of the newspaper on the desk.

5. No one had any idea how long the sandwiches had _____ in the sun or who had _____ them there in the first place.

SIT/SET

Estos dos verbos son muy similares a *lie* y *lay*. *Sit* significa descansar. *Set* significa poner en un lugar. La tabla que sigue muestra las partes principales de cada uno de estos verbos. Sus significados, escritos en la forma correcta, aparecen en paréntesis.

FORMAS DE *SIT* Y *SET*			
Present	**Progressive**	**Past**	**Past Participle***
sit, sits (rest, rests)	sitting (resting)	sat (rested)	sat (rested)
set, sets (put, place; puts, places)	setting (putting, placing)	set (put, placed)	set (put, placed)

El participio pasado es la forma usada conjuntamente con have, has *o* had.

Elija la forma correcta de *sit* o *set* usando, primeramente, el significado de las oraciones (las palabras en paréntesis). Decida cuál significado tiene mejor sentido, y luego elija el verbo correspondiente. Vea cómo esto está hecho en los ejemplos de las oraciones que siguen.

The speaker _____ the chair next to the podium.
   Put o *placed* tiene mejor sentido que *rested*.
   Elija *set*.

The speaker _____ in the chair next to the podium.
   Rested tiene mejor sentido que *put* o *placed*.
   Elija *sat*.

PRÁCTICA

En cada uno de los espacios en blanco, escriba la forma correcta de *sit* o *set*. Las respuestas pueden ser encontradas al final de la lección.

6. The board of directors _____ aside additional money for research and development.

7. My desk is the one _____ closest to the fax machine.

8. I can't remember where I _____ the mail down.

9. I _____ down next to Jill and _____ my briefcase on the chair next to me.

10. We had _____ in the waiting room for almost an hour before the doctor saw us.

RISE/RAISE

El verbo *rise* significa ir hacia arriba. El verbo *raise* significa elevar algo. *Raise* requiere un objeto. En otras palabras, algo tiene que recibir la acción del verbo *raise* (*raise your hand, raise the flag, raise the objection, raise children*). La tabla que sigue muestra las partes principales de ambos verbos.

FORMAS DE *RISE* Y *RAISE*			
Presente	**Progresivo**	**Pasado**	**Pasado Participio***
rises, rise	rising	rose	risen
(goes up, go up)	(going up)	(went up)	(gone up)
(comes up, come up)	(coming up)	(came up)	(come up)
raises, raise	raising	raised	raised
(moves up, move up)	(moving up)	(moved up)	(moved up)

*El participio pasado es la forma usada conjuntamente con have, has *o* had.

Elija la forma correcta de *rise* o *raise* usando, primeramente, el significado de las oraciones (las palabras en paréntesis). Decida qué significado tiene mejor sentido, y luego elija el verbo correspondiente. Vea como esto está hecho en los ejemplos de las oraciones que siguen. A veces, ninguna de las palabras parece ser apropiada. De todas maneras, elija la opción que tiene el mejor significado.

The sun _____ a little bit earlier each day of the spring.
    Comes up tiene más significado.
    Elija *rises*.

Without realizing it, we began to _____ our voices.

    Move up tiene más significado que ninguna otra opción.

    Elija *raise.*

The river _____ over two feet in the last hour.

    Went up tiene más significado.

    Elija *rose.*

PRÁCTICA

En cada uno de los espacios en blanco, escriba la forma correcta de *rise* o *raise.* Las respuestas pueden ser encontradas al final de la lección.

11. The guard _____ the flag every morning before the sun _____.

12. The couple _____ seven of their own children and adopted three more.

13. By late morning the fog had _____ enough for us to see the neighboring farm.

14. The stockholders _____ from their chairs to _____ an objection.

PRONOMBRES PROBLEMÁTICOS

ITS/IT'S

Its es un pronombre posesivo que significa *belonging to it. It's* es la contracción de *it is* o *it has.* La única vez en que va a usar *it's* es cuando usted pueda substituirlo por *it is.* Tome su tiempo en hacer este tipo de substitución, y nunca se equivocará usando estas dos palabras.

    A doe will hide **its** [belonging to the it—the doe] fawn carefully before going out to graze.

    It's [it is] time we packed up and moved to a new location.

    The new computer system has proven **its** [belonging to it] value.

    We'll leave the game as soon as **it's** [it is] over.

YOUR/YOU'RE

Your es un pronombre posesivo que significa *belonging to you. You're* es la contracción de *you are.* La única vez en que va a usar *you're* es cuando usted puede substituirlo por *you are.* Tome su tiempo en hacer este tipo de substitución, y nunca se equivocará usando estas dos palabras.

    Is this **your** [belonging to you] idea of a joke?

    As soon as **you're** [you are] finished, you may leave.

Your [belonging to you] friends are the people you most enjoy.

You're [you are] friends whom we value.

WHOSE/WHO'S

Whose es un pronombre posesivo que significa *belonging to whom*. *Who's* es la contraccción de las palabras *who is* o *who has*. Tome su tiempo para hacer esta substitución, y nunca confundirá estas dos palabras.

Who's [Who is] in charge of the lighting for the show?

Whose [belonging to whom] car was that?

This is the nurse **who's** [who is] on duty until morning.

Here is the man **whose** [belonging to whom] car I ran into this morning.

WHO/THAT/WHICH

Who se refiere a personas. *That* refiere a cosas. *Which* es generalmente usado para introducir cláusulas no restrictivas que describen cosas. (Sobre cláusulas no restrictivas vea la Lección 4.) Estudie las siguientes oraciones para ver cómo cada una de estas palabras es usada.

There is the woman **who** helped me fix my flat tire.

The man **who** invented the polio vaccine died in 1995.

This is the house **that** Jack built.

The book **that** I wanted is no longer in print.

Abigail, **who** rescued my cat from the neighbor's tree, lives across the street.

Yassir Arafat, **who** heads the PLO, met with Israeli leaders.

The teacher asked us to read *Lord of the Flies*, **which** is my favorite novel.

Mt. Massive, **which** is the tallest peak in the Rocky Mountains, looms above Leadville, Colorado.

THERE/THEIR/THEY'RE

There es un adverbio que determina dónde una acción o elementos están localizados. *Their* es un pronombre posesivo que muestra pertenencia. *They're* es la contracción de las palabras *they are*. De todos estos grupos confusos, éste es el que más a menudo se usa incorrectamente. A continuación vea la manera fácil de distinguir entre estas palabras.

- Oberve cuidadosamente esta versión de la palabra: tHERE. Usted puede ver que *there* contiene la palabra *here*. Dondequiera que use la palabra *there*, usted debe poder substituir la palabra *here*, y la oración debe tener sentido.
- *Their* significa *belonging to them*. De las tres palabras, *their* es la que más fácilmente puede transformarse en la palabra *them*. Trate de hacerlo. Descubrirá que las dos pequeñas marcas—conectando la *i* con la *r* y luego trazando una línea para convertir la *ir* en una *m*—transformará *their* en *them*. Este pequeño truco le ayudará a no usar incorrectamente *their*.

■ Finalmente, imagine que la apóstrofe en *they're* es realmente una pequeña letra *a*. Si usted cambia *they're* por *they are* en una oración, nunca usará incorrectamente la palabra. Vea los ejemplos en la siguiente página.

> **There** [here] is my paycheck.
>
> The new chairs are in **there** [here].
>
> **Their** [belonging to them] time has almost run out.
>
> This is **their** [belonging to them] problem, not mine.
>
> **They're** [they are] planning to finish early in the morning.
>
> I wonder how **they're** [they are] going to work this out.

PRÁCTICA

En cada grupo de paréntesis que sigue, encierre la palabra correcta. Las respuestas están al final de la lección.

15. Finally, the dog stopped (its, it's) barking.

16. Alert me when (its, it's) time to go.

17. (Its, It's) time to get a new clock when the old one stops (its, it's) chiming.

18. Take (your, you're) time with this decision.

19. Take (your, you're) samples with you if (your, you're) leaving.

20. (Your, You're) scheduled to work late this evening.

21. (Your, You're) schedule for this evening has changed.

22. My aunt Sophie is the one (who, which, that) travels for a living.

23. This is the book (who, which, that) I lost earlier this year.

24. Kirk Douglas, (who, which, that) is my favorite actor, finally received an Oscar nomination.

25. Redbird Creek, (who, which, that) runs through my back yard, floods every spring.

26. There's the person (who, which, that) gave me directions to the museum.

27. (Your, You're) likely to find the tapes in (there, their, they're).

28. (There, Their, They're) scheduled to begin construction next week.

29. (Its, It's) been over an hour since (there, their, they're) food arrived.

30. The clerk (who, which, that) gave me the estimate is over (there, their, they're).

31. (Who's, Whose) been opening the store in the morning?

32. (Who's, Whose) responsibility is it to open the store in the morning?

33. Hilda spoke to the person (who's, whose) in charge of electronics.

34. (Who's, Whose) birthday is it?

Técnicas de aprendizaje

Identifique el verbo o pronombre especial problemático que le dá más dificultad. Explique a un amigo o miembro de su familia la manera correcta de usarlo. Haga un intento conciente de usarlo correctamente por lo menos tres veces al día.

RESPUESTAS

1. lay
2. Lay
3. lay
4. laid
5. lain, laid
6. set
7. sitting
8. set
9. sat, set
10. sat
11. raised, rose
    or raises, rises

12. raised
13. risen
14. rose, raise
15. its
16. it's
17. It's, its
18. your
19. your, you're
20. You're
21. Your
22. who
23. that

24. who
25. which
26. who
27. You're, there
28. They're
29. It's, their
30. who, there
31. Who's
32. Whose
33. who's
34. Whose

MODIFICADORES

15

RESUMEN DE LA LECCIÓN

Esta lección le enseñará cómo evitar problemas comunes relacionados con el uso de adjetivos y adverbios.

L as palabras y frases que describen otras frases son llamadas *mod-ificadores*. Palabras que describen nombres y pronombres son llamadas *adjetivos*. Palabras que describen verbos, adjetivos, o adverbos son conocidas como *adverbios*. Frases enteras o grupos de palabras pueden también funcionar como modificadores. El idioma inglés está estructurado del tal manera que los modificadores tienen un papel muy importante en la comunicación. Usarlos correctamente es una herramienta importante.

ADJETIVOS

Adjetivos describen un nombre o pronombre en una oración. Ésta es una de las maneras fáciles de determinar si una palabra es un adjetivo. En una oración, los adjetivos contestan una de las tres preguntas sobre otra palabra dentro de la misma oración: ¿cuál? (*which one?*), ¿qué clase? (*what kind?*), y ¿cuánto? (*how many?*). La tabla en la página que sigue ilustra esto. Los adjetivos han sido marcados para que sean fáciles de identificar.

ADJETIVOS		
Which One?	**What Kind?**	**How Many?**
that cubicle	**sports** car	**many** examples
the **other** arrangement	**red** stickers	**three** containers
our **first** project	**wise** mentor	**several** desks

Ponga mucha atención a los adjetivos que siguen a los verbos conectantes. A veces el adjetivo sigue el verbo, pero éste describe un nombre o pronombre que se encuentra antes del verbo. Las oraciones que siguen demuestran este caso. Los adjetivos en itálicas describen el nombre subrayado.

This <u>cheesecake</u> tastes *delicious*. [delicious cheesecake]

Chris's <u>change</u> of heart seemed *appropriate*. [appropriate change]

The <u>room</u> smelled *strange*. [strange room]

FEWER/LESS, NUMBER/AMOUNT

Use el adjetivo *fewer* para modificar nombres en plural, cosas que pueden ser contadas. Use *less* para nombres singulares que representan una cantidad o un grado. La mayoría de los nombres a los cuales se les puede añadir una *s*, requiere el adjetivo *fewer*.

The promotional staff had **fewer** innovative ideas [plural noun] than the marketing staff.

The marketing staff had **less** time [singular noun] to brainstorm than the promotional staff.

El mismo principio es aplicable a los nombres *number* y *amount*. Use el nombre *number* cuando se refiere a cosas que pueden ser convertidas en plurales, que pueden contarse. Use el nombre *amount* cuando se refiere a nombres que están en la forma singular.

The **number** of hours [plural noun] we have for this telethon has been reducido.

The **amount** of time [singular noun] we have for this telethon has been reduced.

ADVERBIOS

Use adverbios para describir verbos, adjetivos, y otros adverbios. Ésta es un manera fácil de determinar si una palabra es un adverbio. Los adverbios contestan una de las preguntas sobre otra palabra en la oración: ¿dónde? (*where?*), ¿cuándo? (*when?*), ¿cómo? (*how?*), y ¿hasta qué punto? (*to what extent?*). Vea la tabla que sigue a continuación. Los adverbios han sido marcados.

Esta otra tabla muestra ejemplos de adverbios que modifican verbos, adjetivos, y otros adverbios. Los adverbios han sido marcados; las palabras que se han modificado están subrayadas.

ADVERBIOS

Where?	When?	How?	To What Extent?
The line moved **forward**.	I saw him **yesterday**.	They spoke **softly**.	I could **hardly** understand.
Store your gear **below**.	Come around **later**.	Cindy types **quickly**.	You **narrowly** missed that car.
Stand **here**.	We'll talk **tonight**.	He sang **happily**.	We **still** won't give in.

ADVERBIOS QUE MODIFICAN

Verbos	Adjetivos	Otros Adverbios
Mail <u>arrives</u> **regularly**.	an **extremely** <u>exciting</u> time	most <u>cleverly</u> presented
Doves <u>sing</u> **mournfully**.	a **hopelessly** <u>difficult</u> problem	quite <u>calmly</u> answered
I <u>responded</u> **immediately**.	an **unusually** <u>sound</u> approach	declined **quite** <u>dramatically</u>

¿ADJETIVO Ó ADVERBIO?

Muy a menudo, los escritores usan erróneamente adjetivos en lugar de adverbios. Usted podrá observar este fenómeno en las oraciones que siguen. Las palabras en itálicas son adjetivos incorrectos usados en lugar de adverbios. La forma adverbial sigue la oración.

Megan can think of answers very *quick*. [**quickly**]
Store these antiques very *careful*. [**carefully**]
Ernie whispered the news as *quiet* as he could. [**quietly**]

Tenga cuidado especial en elegir la palabra correcta cuando use verbos relacionados con los sentidos: tacto, gusto, vista, olfato, y oído. Use un adjetivo si la palabra que sigue el verbo describe un nombre o pronombre que va antes del verbo. En la tabla que sigue, los adjetivos y los adverbios han sido marcados, y los nombres o verbos que los modifican están subrayados.

MODIFICADORES CON VERBOS DE "SENTIDOS"

Adjetivos	Adverbios
The entire <u>group</u> felt **sick** after lunch.	The massage therapist <u>felt</u> **gently** along the patient's spine.
The new <u>keyboard</u> looked **strange** to me.	The detective <u>looked</u> **carefully** at the evidence gathered by the pathologist.
The <u>explanation</u> sounded **plausible** to us.	The biologist <u>smelled</u> the container **gingerly**.

GOOD Y WELL

Good es un adjetivo. *Well* es un adverbio. A veces *good* es erróneamente usado para describir un verbo. Use *well* para describir una acción. En los ejemplos que siguen, las palabras modificadas por *good* y *well* han sido subrayadas.

> Brenton did **well** on the test.
> Raul felt **good** after the marathon.
> The new marketing strategy was **well** planned.
> The lasagna smelled **good** when I walked through the door.

COMPARACIONES

Los adjetivos y adverbios cambian su forma cuando son usados para hacer comparaciones. Cuando usted compara dos cosas, use la forma comparativa del modificador. Si usted está comparando más de dos cosas, use la forma *superlativa* del modificador.

La forma comparativa se puede crear siguiendo una de las dos siguientes maneras:

1. Añada *-er* al modificador si es una palabra corta de una o dos sílabas.

2. Ponga la palabra *more* o la palabra *less* antes del modificador si se trata de una palabra de muchas sílabas.

Además, algunos modificadores cambian su forma completamente. Examine los ejemplos en la tabla que sigue. Las primeras seis líneas de la tabla demuestran la manera en la cual estos modificadores especiales cambian forma. El resto usa las reglas establecidas antetiormente.

MODIFICADORES EN ORACIONES COMPARATIVAS		
Modificador	**Comparativo (dos cosas)**	**Superlativo (más de dos)**
good	better	best
well	better	best
many	more	most
much	more	most
bad	worse	worst
little	less or lesser	least
neat	neater	neatest
lovely	lovelier	loveliest
funny	funnier	funniest
extreme	more [or less] extreme	most [or least] extreme
intelligent	more [or less] intelligent	most [or least] intelligent
precisely	more [or less] precisely	most [or least] precisely

Cuando se comparan cosas en frases preposicionales, use *between* entre dos cosas, y *among* para tres o más. Vea como las formas comparativas y superlativas son usadas en las siguientes oraciones.

Up is the **better** direction for the stock market to be going. [comparing two directions]

Blue looks **better** than any other color we've seen. [comparing two colors many times]

The Buick Park Avenue is the **best** luxury car available. [comparing more than two cars]

The Mississippi is the **best** river for walleye fishing. [comparing more than two rivers]

The first run model was **more thoroughly** tested than the prototype. [comparing two things]

EVITE COMPARACIONES ILÓGICAS Y NO CLARAS

"Ellie is more disorganized than any woman," es una declaración ilógica. Esta oración nos dice que Ellie, quien es una mujer, es más desorganizada que ella misma. Siempre incluya las palabras *other* y *else* para que sus comparaciones puedan mantenerse lógicas.

Ellie is more disorganized than any **other** woman.

Ted can concentrate better than anyone **else** in our division.

EVITE LAS COMPARACIONES DOBLES

Una comparación doble ocurre cuando un escritor usa ambos *-er* o *-est*, y *more* o *most*.

COMPARACIONES DOBLES	
Incorrecto	**Correcto**
Diane is the most friendliest person I know.	Diane is the friendliest person I know.
Judi is less sleepier than I am.	Judi is less sleepy than I am.
The writing in this sample seems more plainer than the writing in the other sample.	The writing in this sample seems plainer than the writing in the other sample.

EVITE EL USO DE NEGATIVOS DOBLES

Cuando una palabra negativa es añadida a una declaración que ya es negativa, se tiene como resultado un negativo doble. Evite los negativos dobles en todo lo que escribe. Las palabras *hardly* y *barely* pueden ocasionar problemas; éstas funcionan como palabras negativas. En los ejemplos que siguen las palabras negativas han sido marcadas. Ponga mucha atención a la manera en la cual las oraciones incorrectas fueron escritas de nuevo para evitar el negativo doble.

NEGATIVOS DOBLES	
Incorrecto	**Correcto**
The warehouse **doesn't** have **no** surplus stock at this time.	The warehouse has **no** surplus stock at this time. The warehouse **doesn't** have any surplus stock at this time.
I **can't hardly** understand this financial report.	I can **hardly** understand this financial report. I **can't** understand this financial report.
The cash on hand **won't barely** cover this expense.	The cash on hand will **barely** cover this expense. The cash on hand **won't** cover this expense.

MODIFICADORES MAL UBICADOS Y COLGANTES

MODIFICADORES MAL UBICADOS

Escriba palabras, frases, o cláusulas que describen nombres y pronombres lo más cerca posible a la palabras que describen. El fallo en hacer esto muy a menudo resulta en un modificador mal ubicado—y en una oración cuyo significado es algo totalmente diferente del intento del autor.

Palabras

Por ejemplo, las palabras *only, almost,* y *just* deben ser ubicadas lo más cerca posible de la palabra que están describiendo. El mejor lugar es inmediatamente antes de la palabra que describen. La ubicación de la palabra afecta el significado de la oración.

> The customers **only** looked at two samples.
> The customers looked at **only** two samples.

En la primera oración arriba, los clientes "only looked" a las muestras; ellos no las tocaron. En la segunda oración los clientes miraron "only two," y no tres o cuatro de las muestras. La ubicación de *only* cambia el significado.
Éste es un ejemplo con *almost.*

> Chad **almost** scored three touchdowns.
> Chad scored **almost** three touchdowns.

En la primera versión, Chad "almost scored" tres veces—él parece que estuvo cerca de la línea de gol tres veces, y en la actualidad sin haberla cruzado. En la segunda versión, Chad logró "almost three" goles—quizás 2. ¿Cuántos puntos son dados por eso?

Es de esta manera que ubicando *just* puede afectar el significado de la oración:

> The Hill family **just** leases a car.
>
> The Hill family leases **just** a car.

En la primera versión, la familia Hill "just leases" un auto, es decir que ellos no son propietarios o han comprado un auto. En la segunda oración, ellos rentan "just a car" y no un camión o una vagoneta u otro vehículo.

Frases y cláusulas

Frases y cláusulas que describen nombres o pronombres deben ser posicionadas tan cerca como sea posible a las palabras que describen. Las siguientes oraciones contienen modificadores mal ubicados. Ponga mucha atención a cómo han sido re-escritos para clarificar su mensaje.

MODIFICADORES MAL UBICADOS	
Incorrecto	**Correcto**
The veterinarian explained how to vaccinate hogs in the community center basement. [Why would you want hogs in the community center?]	In the community center basement, the veterinarian explained how to vaccinate hogs. The veterinarian in the community center basement explained how to vaccinate hogs.
A big dog followed the old man that was barking loudly. [Why was the man barking?]	A big dog that was barking loudly followed the old man. Barking loudly, a big dog followed the old man.

MODIFICADORES COLGANTES

Palabras, frases, o cláusulas que comienzan una oración y son iniciadas con una coma, a veces, por equivocación, modifican al nombre o pronombre incorrecto. Éstos son llamados modificadores colgantes. Las siguientes oraciones contienen modificadores colgantes. Ponga mucha atención a cómo estas oraciones fueron escritas de nuevo para evitar el problema.

PRÁCTICA

En cada una de las siguientes oraciones, encierre en un círculo la palabra correcta. Las repuestas para este grupo de preguntas se encuentra al final del la lección.

1. Greg assembled the desk (correct, correctly).

2. Charlotte seemed (tired, tiredly) after the long plane ride.

3. This drawer doesn't open as (easy, easily) as it used to.

DANGLING MODIFIERS

Wrong	Correct
Flat and useless, Jason removed the bicycle tire. [Why was Jason flat?]	Jason removed the flat and useless bicycle tire. Flat and useless, the bicycle tire was removed by Jason.
Attached to an old stump, Janette saw a No Fishing sign. [Why was Janette attached to an old stump?]	Janette saw a No Fishing sign attached to an old stump. The No Fishing sign attached to an old stump caught Janette's attention.
While cleaning up after dinner, the phone rang. [Don't you wish you had a phone that cleaned up after dinner?]	While I was cleaning up after dinner, the phone rang. While cleaning up after dinner, I heard the phone ring. The phone rang while I was cleaning up after dinner.

4. My new shoes feel more (comfortable, comfortably) than my old ones.

5. Make your request (polite, politely) if you want a positive response.

6. The workers walked (slow, slowly) back to the line after the break.

7. Our team leader seemed (unhappy, unhappily) about something.

8. The passenger on the other side of the bus looked (angry, angrily).

9. The night watchman felt (careful, carefully) for the switch.

10. We looked (thorough, thoroughly) in both locations.

11. You'll have (fewer, less) trouble with this component if you use (fewer, less) joints.

12. The (number, amount) of people we hire will depend on the (number, amount) of time we have to fill the order.

13. Spaghetti tastes especially (good, well) if the noodles are boiled (good, well).

14. Kelly is the (older, oldest) of the twins and the (taller, tallest) one in the whole family.

15. The receiving department hasn't heard (anything, nothing) about the delivery date of our order.

16. Divide these cookies (between, among) the twins, but split the cake (between, among) all the people who come to the party.

De cada uno de los siguientes grupos, elija la oración que ha sido escrita correctamente.

17. a. I like olives and pimentoes boiled in oil.
   b. Boiled in oil, I like olives and pimentos.

18. a. While speeding along a country road, two deer dashed across the road in front of our car.
   b. Two deer dashed across the road in front of our car as we were speeding along a country road.

19. a. At the age of four, my grandmother taught me to read.
   b. When I was four, my grandmother taught me to read.

20. a. We heard about the bank robbers who were arrested on the evening news.
   b. We heard on the evening news about the bank robbers who were arrested.

Técnicas de aprendizaje

Practique lo que usted acaba de aprender en esta lección al escuchar hablar a otras personas. Mucha gente al hablar comete muchos errores con el uso de modificadores. Cuando se dé cuenta de esos errores, piense de qué manera podría escribir de nuevo lo que la persona dijo para corregir estas oraciones. Una vez más, no se sienta obligado a corregir los errores, sólo úselos como un ejercicio mental para que así nadie tenga la oportunidad de corregir lo que usted diga.

RESPUESTAS

1. correctly
2. tired
3. easily
4. comfortable
5. politely
6. slowly
7. unhappy
8. angry
9. carefully
10. thoroughly

11. less, fewer
12. number, amount
13. good, well
14. older, tallest
15. anything
16. between, among
17. a.
18. b.
19. b.
20. b.

PARES DE PALABRAS FÁCILMENTE CONFUNDIDAS

RESUMEN DE LA LECCIÓN

Threw o *through*? *To, two,* o *too*? *Brake* o *break*? Ésta y la próxima lección hacen un repaso de aquellas palabras que son generalmente confundidas con otras; además le mostrará como usted debe usarlas.

Esta lección cubre los pares de palabras que generalmente se confunden en su uso. Si usted aprende a distinguir entre estas palabras, usted puede evitar errors en sus composiciones de escritura. Estas palabras están divididas en tres secciones separadas y contienen ejercicios al final de cada sección. Las palabras en itálicas que siguen algunas frases son sinónimas; palabras que en una oración pueden ser substituidas por las palabras que son confundidas en su uso.

CONFUSIÓN DE TRES MANERAS

LEAD/LED/LEAD

- **Lead** es un verbo que significa *guiar, dirigir*. Como nombre, siginifica *posición frontal*. Esta palabra rima con *seed*.
- **Led** es un verbo, el pasado de **lead**, que significa *guiado* o *dirigido*. Esta palabra rima con *red*.
- **Lead** es un nombre. El *nombre de un metal*. Esta palabra rima con *red*.

Ejemplos:

Gerónimo **led** (*guiaba*) the small band to safety.

We hope the next elected officials will **lead** (*guiarán*) us to economic recovery.

A pound of styrofoam weighs as much as a pound of **lead** (*el metal*).

Jake took the **lead** (*posición frontal*) as the group headed out of town.

QUITE/QUIT/QUIET

- **Quite** es un adverbio que significa *completely, very, entirely*. Esta palabra rima con *fight*.
- **Quit** es un verbo que significa *stop, cease* or *stopped, ceased*. Esta palabra rima con *sit*.
- **Quiet** es un adjetivo que significa *calm, silent, noiseless*. Como verbo significa *soothe, calm*. Como nombre significa *tranquility, peacefulness*. Casi rima con *riot*.

Example:

The firm was **quite** (*muy*) surprised when its most productive investment specialist **quit** (*paró*) work and opted for the **quiet** (*tranquila*) life of a monk.

RIGHT/WRITE/RITE

- **Right** es un adjetivo que significa *correct, proper, opposite of left*.
- **Write** es un verbo que significa *record, inscribe*.
- **Rite** es un nombre que significa *ceremony, ritual*.

Example:

I will **write** (*copiaré*) the exact procedures so you will be able to perform the **rite** (*ceremonia*) in the **right** (*correcta*) way.

SENT/CENT/SCENT

- **Sent** es un verbo, la forma pasada de *send*. Significa *dispatched, transmitted*.
- **Cent** es un nombre que significa *one penny*, una moneda que es un .01 de un dólar.
- **Scent** es un nombre que significa *odor, smell*.

Example:

For a mere **cent** (*un centavo*) I bought an envelope perfumed with the **scent** (*olor*) of jasmine. I **sent** (*envié*) it to my grandmother.

SIGHT/SITE/CITE

- **Sight** como nombre significa *ability to see*. Como verbo significa *see, spot*.
- **Site** es un nombre que significa *location, position*.
- **Cite** es un verbo que significa *quote, make reference to*.

Example:

At ninety-five my grandmother's **sight** (*visión*) was acute enough to **sight** (*ubicar*) even the smallest error in a crocheted doily.

This is the proposed **site** (*ubicación*) for the new building.

You must **cite** (*hacer referencia a*) the source of your information.

TO/TOO/TWO

- **To** es una preposición o parte de un infinitivo. Úsela antes del verbo o sólo para introducir una frase preposicional, que generalmente responde a la pregunta *where*. Use **to** para introducir una frase preposicional: *to the store, to the top, to my home, to our garden, to his laboratory, to his castle, to our advantage, to an open door, to a song, to the science room*, etc. Use **to** como un infinitivo (*to* seguida de un verbo, a veces separada de adverbios): *to run, to jump, to want badly, to seek, to propose, to write, to explode, to sorely need, to badly botch, to carefully examine*, etc.
- **Too** es un adverbio que significa *also, very*.
- **Two** es un adjetivo, *the name of a number*, como en one, two, three.

Ejemplo:

The couple went **to** (*preposición*) the deli **to** (*infinitivo*) pick up **two** (*el número*) plate dinners because both of them were **too** (*muy*) tired **to** (*infinitivo*) cook dinner.

WHERE/WEAR/WERE

- **Where** es un adverbio que se refiere a *place, location*.
- **Wear** es un verbo que significa *put on, tire*. Como nombre significa *deterioration*.
- **Were** como verbo, la forma plural de *be*.

Ejemplos:

The slacks **were** (*forma del verbo ser*) too tight.

The tires showed excessive **wear** (*deterioración*).

They will **wear** (*gastar*) out these shoes if they **wear** (*vestir*) them too much.

Where (*ubicación*) are the clothes you **were** (*forma del verbo ser*) planning to **wear** (*vestir*) tomorrow?

PRÁCTICA

Encierre en un cículo la palabra correcta en los paréntesis que siguen. Las respuestas pueden ser ubicadas al final de la lección.

1. The package will be (sent, cent, scent) if you add another (sent, cent, scent) of postage.

2. We noticed the distinct (sent, cent, scent) of cat litter when we entered the door.

3. Was I (right, write, rite) in assuming I was to (right, write, rite) you a memo about this matter?

4. Who will be performing the (right, write, rite) of baptism at tomorrow's service?

5. If you will simply be (quite, quit, quiet), I will be (quite, quit, quiet) happy to (quite, quit, quiet) annoying you with my constant request for a (quite, quit, quiet) atmosphere in which to work.

6. Our marching band (lead, led) the parade.

7. The drum major, carrying a baton made of (lead, led), will (lead, led) the band.

8. Over the next ridge we will be able to (sight, site, cite) the (sight, site, cite) we've chosen for our new home.

9. I would be honored to have you (sight, site, cite) me in your research.

10. Even though these trousers (where, wear, were) expensive, they are showing (where, wear, were) along the seams.

11. (Where, wear, were) did you buy those earrings?

PALABRAS FÁCILES DE CONFUNDIR

BRAKE/BREAK

- **Brake** como verbo significa *slow, stop*. Como nombre significa *hindrance, drag*.
- **Break** como verbo significa *separate, shatter, adjourn*. Como nombre significa *separation, crack, pause, opportunity*.

Ejemplos:

During our **break** (*pausa*) we spotted a **break** (*rajadura*) in the pipeline.

Brake (*frene*) gently when driving on glare ice by applying slight pressure to the **brake** (*freno*).

PASSED/PAST

- **Passed** es un verbo, la forma pasada de *pass*, que significa *transferred, went ahead or by, elapsed, finished*.
- **Past** como un nombre significa *history*. Como adjetivo significa *former*.

Ejemplos:

The first runner **passed** (*transfirió*) the baton to the second just as she **passed** (*pasó*) the stands. Three seconds **passed** (*transcurrió*) before the next runner came by.

Harriet **passed** (*finalizar*) her bar exam on the first try.

I must have been a whale in a **past** (*anterior, previa, pasada*) life.

Avoid digging up the **past** (*historia*) if you can.

PEACE/PIECE

- **Peace** es un nombre que significa *tranquility*.
- **Piece** como nombre significa *division, creation*. Como verbo significa *patch, repair*.

Ejemplo:

If you can **piece** (*poner en orden*) together the **pieces** (*fragmentos, piezas*) of this story, perhaps we can have some **peace** (*tranquilidad*) around here.

PLAIN/PLANE

- **Plain** como adjetivo significa *ordinary, clear, simple*. Como nombre, se refiere *flat country*, también comunmente es escrito como **plains.**
- **es un nombre que significa** *airship* o *flat surface*. Es ocasionalmente usado como verbo o adjetivo que significa *level*.

Ejemplos:

They wore **plain** (*ordinaria, común*) clothes.

It was **plain** (*claro, obvio*) to see.

The meal we ate on the **plains** (*llanura*) was quite **plain** (*simple*).

It was **plain** (*claro, obvio*) to us that the enemy did not see our **plane** (*avión, aeroplano*) sitting on the open **plain** (*llanura*).

SCENE/SEEN

- **Scene** es un nombre que significa *view, site, commotion*.
- **Seen** es un verbo, el pasado participio de *see*, que significa *observed, noticed*.

Ejemplo:

We caused quite a **scene** (*conmoción*) at the **scene** (*lugar*) of the accident. It was the worst we had ever **seen** (*observado*).

THREW/THROUGH

- **Threw** es un verbo, la forma pasada de *throw*, que significa *tossed*.
- **Through** es un adverbio o una preposición que significa *in one side and out the other*. Use **through** para presentar una frase preposicional: *through the door, through the lobby, though the mist*.

Ejemplo:

Fred **threw** (*arrojó*) the ball **through** (*a través*) the hoop.

WEAK/WEEK

- **Weak** es un adjetivo que significa *flimsy, frail, powerless.*
- **Week** es un nombre que significa *a period of seven days.*

Ejemplo:

The patient's heartbeat was so **weak** (*frágil*) that the doctor was certain he would be dead within a **week** (*siete días*).

WHICH/WITCH

- **Which** es un pronombre relacionado con *choice.* Como adverbio introduce una cláusula subordinada.
- **Witch** es un nombre que significa *sorceress, enchantress.*

Ejemplos:

Which (*elección, preferencia*) one do you want?

This car, **which** (*introduce una cláusula subordinada*) I have never driven, is the one I'm thinking about buying.

I don't know **which** (*elección, preferencia*) **witch** (*bruja, maga*) I should consult about my future.

PRÁCTICA

Encierre en un círculo la forma correcta de las siguientes palabras en paréntesis. Las respuestas pueden ser encontradas al final de la lección.

12. (Which, Witch) (which, witch) scares you the most?

13. Gerald (threw, through) away his opportunity when he walked (threw, through) the door.

14. Sally slammed on the (brake, break) when she saw the car ahead (brake, break) to avoid the (brake, break) in the concrete road.

15. Have you (scene, seen) that pathetic (scene, seen) in the movie?

16. The confused (which, witch) couldn't decide (which, witch) broomstick to use on Halloween.

17. The sales department has (passed, past) the record it had established in the (passed, past) year.

18. We'll need at least a (weak, week) to repair the (weak, week) linkage in this machine.

19. This (peace, piece) of news should give you some (peace, piece) of mind.

20. The (plain, plane) brown packages were loaded on the (plain, plane).

Separar o no separar

ALREADY/ALL READY

- **Already** es un adverbio que significa *as early as this, previously, by this time.*
- **All ready** significa *completely ready, totally ready.*

Ejemplos:

At age four, Brigitta is reading **already** (*tan temprano como*).

We had **already** (*anteriormente, hasta esta fecha*) finished.

Are we **all ready** (*completamente listos*) to go?

ALTOGETHER/ALL TOGETHER

- **Altogether** es un adverbio que significa *entirely, completely.*
- **All together** significa *simultaneously.*

Ejemplos:

These claims are **altogether** (*enteramente, completamente*) false.

The audience responded **all together** (*enteramente, completamente*).

EVERYDAY/EVERY DAY

- **Everyday** enteramente, completamente *ordinary, usual.*
- **Every day** significa *each day.*

Ejemplos:

These are our **everyday** (*comunes, usuales*) low prices.

The associates sort the merchandise **every day** (*cada día*).

MAYBE/MAY BE

- **Maybe** es un adverbio que significa *perhaps.*
- **May be** es una frase verbal que significa *might be.*

Ejemplo:

Maybe (*quizás*) the next batch will be better than this one. On the other hand, it **may be** (*puede ser*) worse.

SIEMPRE SEPARE

- **All right.** No hay una palabra como *alright* a pesar de que muchas veces la va a ver escrita de esta manera.
- **A lot.** No hay una palabra como *alot*. Hay una palabra *allot*, pero significa *la parte de algo.*

Ejemplo:

I thought it was **all right** that we **allotted** tickets to **a lot** of our best customers.

PRÁCTICA

Encierre en un círculo la palabra correcta de los paréntesis que siguen.

21. I (where, wear, were) my (everyday, every day) clothes almost (everyday, every day).

22. (Maybe, may be) we should design a new model. It (maybe, may be) just the thing to brighten our financial picture.

23. If you had been (already, all ready), we could have (already, all ready) begun.

24. You'll be (alright, all right) if you follow the instructions.

25. When the staff is (altogether, all together), we should have (altogether, all together) enough brainpower for this project.

Técnicas de aprendizaje

Vea cuántas de estas palabras fáciles de confundir puede usted identificar en sus lecturas. Trate de substituirlas por los sinónimos que acaba de aprender.

RESPUESTAS

1. sent, cent	**7.** lead, lead	**14.** brake, brake, break	**21.** wear, everyday, every day
2. scent	**8.** sight, site	**15.** seen, scene	**22.** Maybe, may be
3. right, write	**9.** cite	**16.** witch, which	**23.** all ready, already
4. rite	**10.** were, wear	**17.** passed, past	**24.** all right
5. quiet, quite, quit, quiet	**11.** Where	**18.** week, weak	**25.** all together, altogether
6. led	**12.** Which, witch	**19.** piece, peace	
	13. threw, through	**20.** plain, plane	

17

PARES DE PALABRAS MÁS FÁCILMENTE CONFUNDIDAS

RESUMEN DE LA LECCIÓN

Algunas de las palabras más comunmente usadas en el idioma inglés son usualmente confundidas con otras igualmente comunes. Para evitar confusión en sus lectores, usted tiene que saber cuáles son estas palabras.

Esta lección cubre una gran parte de aquellos pares de palabras usualmente mal usados al escribir. Si usted aprende a reconocer estas palabras, puede evitar cometer errors. Las palabras están divididas en tres secciones separadas, cada una con ejercicios de prácticas al final de las mismas. Las palabras en itálicas son sinónimos, palabras que pueden substituir a las palabras mal usadas dentro de la oración.

PEQUEÑA PERO DESAFIANTE

BY/BUY

- **By** es una preposición usada para introducir una frase (by the book, by the time, by the way)
- **Buy** como verbo significa *purchase*. Como nombre, significa *bargain, deal.*

  Ejemplos:

    We stopped **by** *(preposición)* the store to **buy** *(compra)* some groceries.

    That car was a great **buy** *(compra, oferta).*

DEAR/DEER

- **Dear** es un adjetivo que significa *valued, loved*.
- **Deer** es un nombre que se refiere a un *animal*, de cuatro patas que vive en el bosque y que se parece a Bambi.
  Ejemplo:

  The **dear** *(amado)* man died when his car struck a **deer** *(animal)*.

DIE/DYE

- **Die** es un verbo que significa *pass away, fade*.
- **Dye** como verbo significa *color, tint*. Como nombre, se refiere a *coloring, pigment*.
  Ejemplo:

  We waited for the wind to **die** *(disminuir)* before we decided to **dye** *(color)* the sheets.

HEAR/HERE

- **Hear** es un verbo que significa *listen to*.
- **Here** como verbo significa *in this place, to this place*.
  Ejemplo:

  Please come **here** *(a este lugar)* so you can **hear** *(escuchar)* what I have to say.

HOLE/WHOLE

- **Hole** es un nombre que significa *opening, gap*.
- **Whole** como adjetivo significa *entire, intact*. Como nombre significa *entire part or amount*.
  Ejemplos:

  The **whole** *(completo)* group heard the message.
  They patched the **hole** *(apertura, hoyo)* in the wall.

KNEW/NEW

- **Knew** es un verbo, la forma pasada de *know*. Significa *understood, recognized*.
- **New** es un adjetivo que significa *fresh, different, current*.
  Ejemplo:

  I **knew** *(entendí)* they were planning to buy a **new** *(diferente)* car.

KNOW/NO

- **Know** es un verbo que significa *understand, recognize*.
- **No** como adverbio significa *not so, not at all*. Como adjetivo significa *none, not one*.
  Ejemplo:

  As far as I **know** *(entiendo)*, we have **no** *(ninguno)* more of these shoes in stock.

MEAT/MEET

- **Meat** es un nombre que significa *food, flesh, main part.*
- **Meet** como verbo significa *assemble, greet, fulfill.* Como nombre significa *assembly.*

   Examples:

   Before a track **meet** *(asamblea, competencia),* it is better to eat foods high in carbohydrates rather than **meat** *(carne).*

   The **meat** *(parte principal)* of his message was that our efforts did not **meet** *(alcanzar)* his standards.

ONE/WON

- **One** puede ser un adjetivo que significa *single.* Puede ser también un pronombre usado para identificar una cosa o persona.
- **Won** es un verbo, el pasado de *win.* Significa *prevailed, achieved, acquired.*

   Example:

   Jacquez is the **one** *(pronombre que se refiere a Jack)* who **won** *(logró)* the most improved bowler trophy this year.

SEAM/SEEM

- **Seam** es un nombre que significa *joint, joining point.*
- **Seem** es un verbo que significa *appear.*

   Example:

   Does it **seem** *(aparecer)* to you as if this **seam** *(costura)* is weakening?

PRÁCTICA

Encierre en un círculo la forma correcta de las siguientes palabras en paréntesis. Las respuestas pueden ser encontradas al final de la lección.

1. If the copier isn't repaired (by, buy) noon, we'll need to (by, buy) a new one.

2. (By, Buy) this book that was written (by, buy) a well-known expert on the subject. It's a great (by, buy).

3. The (dear, deer) I had as a pet was quite (dear, deer) to me.

4. The sound began to (die, dye) during the most exciting part of the movie.

5. How do I (die, dye) this shirt?

6. If you sit (hear, here), you'll be able to (hear, here) much better.

7. We can see the (hole, whole) field through this little (hole, whole).

8. I wish I (knew, new) how to operate this (knew, new) equipment.

9. You (know, no) we have (know, no) idea how to solve this problem.

10. After a kill, a pride of lions will (meat, meet) so each can get a share of the (meat, meet).

11. The Colts (one, won) the game by just (one, won) point.

12. I (seam, seem) to be unable to locate the (seam, seem) in this pipe.

PALABRAS COMUNMENTE USADAS Y USADAS MAL

CHOOSE/CHOSE

- **Choose** es un verbo que significa *select*. Rima con *bruise*.
- **Chose** es el pasado de *choose;* significa *selected*. Rima con *hose*.
  Ejemplo:
  Henry **chose** *(eligió)* flex hours on Friday afternoons. I will **choose** *(elegir)* the same option.

LOOSE/LOSE/LOSS

- **Loose** es un adjetivo que significa *free, unrestrained, not tight*. Rima con *goose*.
- **Lose** es un verbo que significa *misplace, to be defeated, fail to keep*. Rima con *shoes*.
- **Loss** es un nombre que significa *defeat, downturn,* lo opuesto *victory* or *gain*. Rima con *toss*.
  Ejemplos:
  The chickens ran **loose** *(libre)* in the yard.
  The knot holding the boat to the dock was **loose** *(no seguro)*.
  Where did you **lose** *(perdiste)* your gloves?
  The investors will **lose** *(perder)* considerable capital if the market suffers a **loss** *(downturn)*.

SUPPOSE/SUPPOSED

- **Suppose** es un verbo que significa *assume, imagine*.
- **Supposed** es un verbo en la forma pasada de *suppose* y significa *assumed, imagined*. Como un adjetivo significa *expected, obligated*.
  Ejemplos:
  I **suppose** *(supongo)* you'll be late, as usual.
  We all **supposed** *(suponimos)* you would be late.
  You were **supposed** *(supuesto)* to have picked up the copies of the report before you came to the meeting.

THAN/THEN

- **Than** es una palabra de conjunción usada para hacer comparaciones.
- **Then** es un adverbio referente a *when* o que significa *next*.

  Ejemplo:

  Then *(seguidamente)*, the group discussed the ways in which the new procedures worked better *than* *(conjunción haciendo comparación)* the old.

USE/USED

- **Use** como verbo significa *utilize, deplete*. Rima con *ooze*. Como nombre, rima con *goose* y significa *purpose*.
- **Used** como verbo es la forma pasada de *use* y significa *utilized, depleted*. Como adjetivo significa *second-hand*.
- **Used to** puede ser usado como un adjetivo, significa *accustomed to*, o como un adverbio que significa *formerly*. (Note que nunca se debe escribir *use to* cuando lo que quiere decir es *accustomed to* o *formerly*.)

  Ejemplos:

  Just **use** *(use)* the same password we **used** *(usamos)* yesterday.

  What's the **use** *(propósito)* in trying yet another time?

  We should consider buying **used** *(de segunda mano)* equipment.

  We **used to** *(anteriormente)* require(*d*) a second opinion.

  Residents of Buffalo, New York, are **used to** *(acostumbrados)* cold temperatures.

WEATHER/WHETHER

- **Weather** es un nombre que se refiere a *condition outside*.
- **Whether** es un adverbio usado cuando se trata de una *possibility*.

  Ejemplos:

  The **weather** *(condición externa)* took a turn for the worse.

  Let me know **whether** *(una posibilidad)* you are interested in this new system.

PRÁCTICA

Encierre en un círculo la forma correcta de las siguientes palabras en paréntesis. Las respuestas pueden ser encontradas al final de la lección.

13. If you (choose, chose) your words carefully, you can avoid offending anyone else.

14. The committee (choose, chose) the model with the most special features.

15. The (loose, lose, loss) caused the stockholders to (loose, lose, loss) confidence in the company.

16. How could you (loose, lose, loss) your temper over such a trivial matter?

17. The paper tray seems (loose, lose, loss) to me.

18. I (suppose, supposed) you thought I was the one who was (suppose, supposed) to speak at the banquet.

19. Add even more sugar (than, then) you already have, and (than, then) stir the mixture thoroughly.

20. We found yet another (use, used) for the (use, used) tires that (use, used) to be stacked outside the building.

21. Do you know (weather, whether) this beautiful (weather, whether) is (suppose, supposed) to continue into the weekend?

LAS INDOMABLES *A*'S Y *AL*'S

ACCEPT/EXCEPT/EXPECT

- **Accept** es un verbo que significa *receive, bear.*
- **Except** es una preposición que significa *but, excluding.*
- **Expect** es un verbo que significa *anticipate, demand, assume.*
  Ejemplos:
  This client **expects** *(demanda)* nothing **except** *(pero)* the most sophisticated options available.
  Will you **accept** *(hacerse cargo de)* the responsibility for this decision?
  We **expect** *(anticipar)* everyone to come **except** *(excluyendo)* John.

ADVICE/ADVISE

- **Advice** es un nombre que significa *suggestion, suggestions.* Rima con *ice.* (Ayuda: Piense en *adv*ICE.)
- **Advise** es un verbo que significa *suggest to, warn.* Rima con *wise.*
  Ejemplos:
  We **advise** *(sugerimos)* you to proceed carefully.
  That was the best **advice** *(sugerencia, consejo)* I've received so far.

AFFECT/EFFECT

- **Affect** es un verbo que significa *alter, inspire or move emotionally, imitate.* **Affected,** además de ser la forma pasada de *affect,* puede también ser usado como un adjetivo que significa *imitated, pretentious.*
- **Effect** como nombre significa *consequence.* Como verbo significa *cause.*
  Ejemplos:
  How will this plan **affect** *(altera)* our jobs? What **effect** *(consecuencia)* will this restructuring have on profits? Will it **effect** *(causa)* an increase?
  The movie **affected** *(motivar emocionalmente)* Marian.

He **affected** *(imitar)* an English accent.

The **affected** *(pretencioso)* speech fooled no one.

CAPITAL/CAPITOL

- **Capital** como nombre significa *assets* como también *the city that is the seat of government.* Como adjetivo significa *main, very important,* or *deserving of death.*
- **Capitol** es un nombre que se refiere a *the building that houses the government.*
  Ejemplos:
  How much **capital** *(capital, monto principal)* are you willing to invest?

  I think that's a **capital** *(principal)* objective.

  First degree murder is a **capital** *(pena de muerte)* crime.

  Albany is the **capital** *(capital)* of New York.

  No legislators were injured in the explosion in the **capitol** *(edificio)*.

PERSONAL/PERSONNEL

- **Personal** es un adjetivo que significa *private.*
- **Personnel** es un nombre que significa *staff, employees* o un adjetivo que significa *dealing with staff or employees.*
  Ejemplos:
  The director of **personnel** *(empleados)* keeps all the **personnel** *(empleados)* files in order and guards any **personal** *(privado)* information they contain.

PRINCIPAL/PRINCIPLE

- **Principal** como nombre se refiere al *head of a school* o a una *investment.* Como un adjetivo significa *primary, major.*
- **Principle** es un nombre que significa *rule, law, belief.*
  Ejemplos:
  The **principal** *(director)* of Calbert High School used the **principal** *(inversión)* of an endowment fund to cover this month's salaries.

  The **principal** *(principal)* objective is to make decisions that are in keeping with our **principles** *(creencias)*.

PRÁCTICA

Encierre en un círculo la forma correcta de las siguientes palabras en paréntesis. Las respuestas pueden ser encontradas al final de la lección.

22. Surely you didn't (accept, except, expect) Weldon to (accept, except, expect) responsibility for this decision when everyone (accept, except, expect) him was consulted.

23. We (accept, except, expect) the delivery to arrive early in the morning.

24. The soothsayer will (advice, advise) you to seek her (advice, advise) often.

25. The new work schedule (affected, effected) production in a positive way.

26. How will this new work schedule (affect, effect) production?

27. What (affect, effect) will this new work schedule have on production?

28. We plan to tour the (capital, capitol) building whenever we visit a state's (capital, capitol) city.

29. We never release (personal, personnel) information about our (personal, personnel).

30. The employees' (principal, principle) concern is workload.

31. The new legislation violates the basic (principals, principles) upon which the country was founded.

Técnicas de aprendizaje

Haga un esfuerzo conciente de usar las formas correctas de estas plabras que fácilmente se confunden en la escritura. Puede que encuentre muy ventajoso el copiar las palabras y sus sinónimos en una hoja de papel aparte. Esto le proveerá con un buen repaso y le servirá como referencia que usted pueda usar cuando escriba.

RESPUESTAS

1. by, buy
2. Buy, by, buy
3. deer, dear
4. die
5. dye
6. here, hear
7. whole, hole
8. knew, new
9. know, no
10. meet, meat
11. won, one
12. seem, seam
13. choose
14. chose
15. loss, lose
16. lose
17. loose
18. suppose, supposed
19. than, then
20. use, used, used
21. whether, weather, supposed
22. expect, accept, except
23. expect
24. advise, advice
25. affected
26. affect
27. effect
28. capitol, capital
29. personal, personnel
30. principal
31. principles

DICCIÓN

18

RESUMEN DE LA LECCIÓN

Seguro que usted está pensando; "¿dicción, en un libro de escritura?. *La dicción* no sólo se refiere a la manera en que las palabras son pronunciadas sino también a qué palabras uno elije al hablar. Para el uso efectivo del lenguaje, los escritores tienen que escribir concisa y precisamente. Esta lección y la lección 19 se enfocan en este aspecto; cómo elegir las palabras que mejor comunican lo que quiere decir.

Una palabra es algo que no se puede desperdiciar. Mejor dicho, "Es algo terrible el desperdiciar una palabra." La diferencia entre estas dos versiones es una selección de dicción, el uso apropiado de palabras para combinarlas de la mejor manera para comunicar precisamente un mensaje. Esta lección presenta maneras de evadir algunas de las trampas más frecuentes de la dicción: demasiadas palabras, falta de precisión, coloquialismos y clichés. Aprender a reconocer y evadir esas debilidades en la escritura, convierte a un escritor mediocre en un buen escritor—esto significa el expresar ideas de la *mejor* y *más clara* manera posible.

ELOCUENCIA

Excesivas palabras en la comunicación pierden espacio y tiempo. No sólo eso, pero pueden llegar a distorcionar el mensaje o hacer dificultoso que el lector entienda lo que esté leyendo. Haga hábito de reducir su escritura, haciendo que las oraciones sean lo más concisas posible. Si usted usa cinco palabras cuando tres son suficientes, borre las palabras extras o construya una oración donde excluye estas palabras. Vea si puede escribir de nuevo las oraciones de la primera columa y dé más significado a sus oraciones. Revise y compare su versión con áquella de la segunda columna.

Original	Revisada
It was a three-hour period after the accident when the rescue squad that we knew was going to help us arrived. [21 words]	The rescue squad arrived three hours after the accident. [9 words]
It was decided that the church would organize a committee for the purpose of conducting a search for a new pastor. [21 words]	The church organized a committee to search for a new pastor. [11 words]

Las palabras adicionales de la primera columna no añaden información. Todo lo que hacen es ocupar más espacio.

PALABRAS BULLICIOSAS Y MODIFICADORES VACIOS

Palabras bulliciosas como *aspect, element, factor, scope, situation, type, kind, forms,* y otras más, suenan muy importantes, pero no suman importancia a una oración. Generalmente señalan a un escritor que tiene poco o casi nada que decir, pero que desea sonar importante. De la misma manera, modificadores como *absolutely, definitely, really, very, important, significant, current, major,* y *quite* pueden sumar la extención de una oración, pero muy raramente sumar contenido o significado.

Original Larga

The *nature of the* scheduling system is a *very important matter* that can *definitely* have a *really significant* impact on the morale *aspect* of an employee's attitude. *Aspects of* our current scheduling policy make it *absolutely necessary* that we undergo a *significant* change.

Revisada

The scheduling system can affect employee morale. Our policy needs to be changed.

Las siguiente tabla contiene un grupo de frases que pueden ser reducidas a una o dos palabras.

Original Larga	Consisa	Original Larga	Consisa
puzzling in nature	puzzling	at this point in time	now, today
of a peculiar kind	peculiar	at that point in time	then
regardless of the fact that	although	in order to	to
due to the fact that	because	by means of	by
of an indefinite nature	indefinite	exhibits a tendency to	tends to
concerning the matter of	about	in connection with	with
in the event that	if	in relation to	with

VOZ PASIVA

El uso de la voz pasiva ocaciona oraciones largas que pueden ser corregidas usando verbos en la voz activa. (Vea la lección 11 si no recuerda la voz pasiva.)

Pasiva	Activa
It has been decided that your application for grant money is not in accordance with the constraints outlined by the committee in the application guidelines.	The committee denied your grant because it did not follow the application guidelines.
The letter of resignation was accepted by the Board of Directors.	The Board of Directors accepted the resignation.

INTELECTUALISMO

Las anteriores oraciones pasivas sufren no solamente por ser largas, sino también porque el escritor trata de hacer que su escritura suene intelectual, para hacer que el mensaje suene más difícil de lo que realmente necesita ser. Muchos escritores cometen este error de muchas maneras. Una de estas es convertir adjetivos y verbos en nombres. Esta transformación generalmente significa que palabras extras son añadidas a la oración.

Original Verbosa	Revisada
Water *pollution* [noun] is not as serious in the northern parts of Canada.	Water is not as *polluted* [adjective] in northern Canada.
Customer *demand* [noun] is reducing in the area of sales services.	Customers *demand* [verb] fewer sales services.

Otra manera en la cual escritores añaden palabras sin un mensaje importante es el usar un tono pretencioso. A continuación, se presenta un ejemplo de un comunicado que un burócrata envió durante la Segunda Guerra Mundial. Cuando fue enviado para que el Presidente Franklin Roosevelt lo aprobara, éste lo editó. El mensaje original y la edición de Roosevelt son presentados a continuación.

Original comunicado pretensioso:

In the unlikely event of an attack by an invader of a foreign nature, such preparations shall be made as will completely obscure all Federal buildings and non-Federal buildings occupied by the Federal government during an air raid for any period of time from visibility by reason of internal or external illumination.

Comunicado editado por Roosevelt:

If there is an air raid, put something across the windows and turn off the lights outside in buildings where we have to keep the work going.

Este es otro ejemplo de un mensaje pretensioso, y su versión revisada.

Comunicado Pomposo:

As per the most recent directive issued from this office, it is incumbent upon all employees and they are henceforth instructed to reduce in amount the paper used in the accomplishment of their daily tasks due to the marked increase in the cost of such supplies.

Revisado:

Since paper costs have increased, employees must use less paper.

ECONOMÍA DE PALABRAS

Oración Alargada	Oración Concisa
Cassandra seems to be content.	Cassandra seems content.
We must know what it is that we are doing.	We must know what we're doing.
This is the book of which I have been speaking.	I spoke about this book.
It is with pleasure that I announce the winner.	I am pleased to announce the winner.
The reason we were late was because of traffic.	We were late because of traffic.
These plans will be considered on an individual basis.	These plans will be considered individually.
The caterer, who was distressed, left the party.	The distressed caterer left the party.
There are new shipments arriving daily.	New shipments arrive daily.
Due to the fact that we were late, we missed the door prizes.	We came late and missed the door prizes.
The consideration given in the latest promotion is an example of how I was treated unfairly.	I was not fairly considered for the latest promotion.

Algunas veces, escritores alargan sus oraciones con palabras innecesarias, todo con el propósito de sonar inteligentes. La tabla en la página previa, ilustra oraciones alargadas y cómo pudieron ser escritas más concisamente.

REDUNDANCIA

Otra trampa de escritura que ocupa espacio es la redundancia, el repetir palabras que expresan la misma idea o en las cuales el significado se repite. Si usted se pone a pensar en las frases que siguen a continuación—y muchas otras—verá que las palabras extras no sólo son innecesarias y tontas.

enclosed *with this letter*	continue *on*, proceed *ahead*
remit *payment*	repeated *over again*
absolutely necessary	gather *together*
weather *outside*	*compulsory* requirement
postpone *until later*	*temporarily* suspended
refer *back*	*necessary* requirements
past history	plain *and simple*
ask *the question*	

Enclosed significa que está dentro la carta, ¿no es cierto? *Remit* significa *pay*. Y ¿cómo puede ser algo más *necessary* que *necessary*? ¿El tiempo *outside* opuestamente al tiempo *inside*? ¿*Past* history opuestamente a ...? Se da cuenta. Trate de mantener sus oraciones simples. (No *plain and simple*.)

PRÁCTICA

Trate de escribir de nuevo las siguientes oraciones para omitir las oraciones innecesarias. Las revisions sugeridas se encuentran al final de esta lección, pero puede que usted llegue a escribir versiones diferentes. Hay más de una manera de escribir las oraciones.

1. Stephanie is a very important employee who has played a significant role in the success of this company.

2. Some educators hold with the opinion that corporal punishment should in fact be reinstated in our schools to act as a deterrent to those students who are considering engaging in inappropriate behavior.

3. It is certainly a true statement that bears repeating over and over again that technological advancements such as computers can assist employees in performing in a very efficient manner, and that these self-same computers may in fact result in considerable savings over a period of time.

4. I arrived at a decision to allow the supervisor of my department to achieve a higher golf score in order to enhance my opportunities for advancement in the event that such opportunities became available.

LENGUAJE PRECISO

Practique hasta lograr que su escritura sea lo más precisa possible. Al hacer esto, verá cómo logra comunicar más significado con pocas palabras. En otras palabras, logrará que su escritura sea más concisa. Elija los verbos, modificadores, y nombres exactos que le ayuden a transmitir un significado exacto.

IMPRECISO VS. PRECISO	
Verbos	
Emilia participated in the protest.	Emilia organized the march on the capital.
Hannah won't deal with sales meetings.	Hannah won't attend sales meetings.
Dick can relate to Jane.	Dick understands Jane's feelings.
Modificadores	
These bad instructions confused me.	These disorganized, vague instructions left me with no idea how to repair the leak.
Toy Story is a good movie with fun for all.	*Toy Story* is a clever animated film with humor, adventure, and romance.
We had a nice time with you.	We enjoyed eating your food, drinking your wine, and swimming in your pool.
Nombres	
I always have trouble with this computer.	I can never get this computer to save or to print.
I like to have fun when I take a vacation.	I like to swim, fish, and eat out when I'm on vacation.
Let me grab some things from my locker.	Let me grab my purse and books from my locker.

ABSTRACTO VS. CONCRETO

El lenguaje abstracto se refiere a ideas intangibles o a grupos de personas o cosas en lugar de referirse a la misma gente o cosas. Las abstracciones se basan en ideas concretas. Sin tener un manejo del significado concreto, no se puede esperar que un lector entienda una idea abstracta. Cuando periodistas y abogados escriben, están al tanto de las diferencias entre lo abstracto y lo concreto. Su meta es presentar los hechos claramente, para que el lector pueda llegar a sus propias conclusiones. Tratan de evitar hacer suposiciones para el lector, y esperan que los hechos hablen por sí mismos. Un lenguaje concreto requiere más tiempo y concentración pero comunica un mensaje más efectivamente. Palabras adicionales son una ventaja sólo si añaden al significado o aumentan la precisión.

Suposición Abstracta	Detalles Concretos
Strader was drunk.	Strader smelled strongly of alcohol, slurred his words when he spoke, and stumbled often as he walked.
The couple was in love.	The couple held hands, kissed often, hugged, and ignored everything around them.
Billie is reliable and responsible.	Billie always arrives on time, completes her assignments, and helps others if she has time.

CLICHÉS

Un cliché es un frase muy comunmente y frecuentemente usada que quita toda originalidad de algo escrito. Éstas son frases clichés: *a needle in a haystack, quiet as a mouse, crack of dawn, tough as nails, naked truth, hear a pin drop,* y muchas otras. Algunos escritores usan estas frases cuando no tienen el tiempo ni la habilidad de crear un lenguaje más preciso y de mayor significado. Pese a que los clichés son como mensajes abreviados, se apoyan en pensamientos estereo típicos para comunicar un mensaje. Si el mensaje es importante, un lenguaje fresco y nuevo logrará hacer una impresión más fuerte que aquellas frases o palabras muy usadas. Un lenguaje original estimula el pensamiento y eleva la concentración del lector. Aún más, una imagen fresca es un aliciente para el lector que está poniendo atención a lo que usted ha escrito.

Imagine que un escritor quiso explicar lo difícil que fue encontrar el origen de un problema. Vea las dos versiones presentadas a continuación. Una de ellas se apoya en el uso de clichés para comunicar su mensaje mientras que la otra usa un método nuevo y más original. ¿Qué versión es más probable que haga una impresión más fuerte y que comunique el mensaje más efectivamente?

Finding the source of this problem was harder than finding a needle in a haystack.
Finding the source of this problem was harder than finding a fact in a political advertisement.

Éstos son dos ejemplos más que contrastan los clichés y frases originales. Note las diferencias. Cuando usted revise su escritura, busque la manera de reemplazar palabras y frases comunmente usadas con otras que sean frescas y originales.

We rose at the crack of dawn.
We rose with the roosters.

Having Sam at our negotiations meetings was like having a loose cannon on deck.
Having Sam at our negotiations meetings was like having a German shepherd's tail in your crystal closet.

JERGA

La jerga es el lenguaje técnico idiomático de aquéllos asociados por un oficio o una profesión. Generalmente está lleno de voz pasiva, abreviaciones, términos técnicos y palabras abstractas. Los escritores usan la jerga con la intención de sonar educados, sofisticados o conocedores. En la práctica, la jerga oscurece o incluso distorciona el mensaje. Compare los siguientes párrafos.

Alex demonstrates a tendency to engage inappropriately in verbal social interaction during class time. His grades are deficient because he suffers from an unwillingness to complete supplementary assignments between class periods.

Alex talks in class when he isn't supposed to. He has low grades because he doesn't do his homework.

El primer párrafo nos da la impresión de que Alex es un sociápata con un problema muy serio. El segundo lo pinta como un estudiante que necesita hablar menos y trabajar más. Cuando usted escriba, trate de lograr claridad con un lenguaje que exactamente comunique su mensaje. Una comunicación clara deja una mejor impresión que una pretenciosa, abstracta, y llena de palabras de jerga.

PRÁCTICA

Elija la opción que exprese más clara y concisamente la idea. Las respuestas se pueden encontrar al final de la lección.

5. a. On June 17, Dr. Sam Boswell and Ms. Lorene Webb had an argument over a parking space in the Eagle Supermarket parking lot. Police officers told them both to go home instead of arresting them.
   b. On or about June 17, in the Eagle Supermarket parking lot, Dr. Sam Boswell and Ms. Lorene Webb were allegedly involved in an altercation over a parking space. The police were called. There were no arrests. Both parties were advised to go home by the police officers.

6. a. The most expeditious option in a situation such as this is inevitably also the most advantageous option.

   b. The fastest way is the best way.

7. a. Too many television viewers prefer mindless entertainment to thought-provoking programs.

   b. Too many television viewers prefer "Gilligan's Island" to "The MacNeil-Lehrer Report."

8. a. The research department found that customers are not satisfied with our magazines.

   b. Consumer attitude studies by the research department clearly indicated an extremely low level of customer satisfaction with regard to our newsstand products.

Técnicas de aprendizaje

Escuche a gente del gobierno mientras éstos dan un mensaje. ¿Hablan clara y simplemente o están tratando de sonar "oficial"? Un escritor o orador competente no necesita una máscara de lenguaje pretencioso o abstracto y que suene sofisticado.

RESPUESTAS

1. Stephanie has contributed a lot to this company's success.
2. Some educators believe that unruly students should be spanked.
3. Using computers can save time and money.
4. I let my supervisor beat me at golf so that she would promote me.

5. a.
6. b.
7. b.
8. a.

L · E · C · C · I · Ó · N
MÁS SOBRE DICCIÓN
19

RESUME DE LA LECCIÓN

Esta lección continua con las ideas presentadas en la anterior: el escribir y comunicarse efectivamente. Esta lección cubre temas relacionados con el coloquialismo, lenguaje cargado, punto de vista consistente, paralelismo, y lenguaje genérico neutral.

Los buenos escritores saben que la comunicación requiere la elección cuidadosa de palabras . Los lectores evitan estilos de escritura que sean muy formales, demasiado informales, inapropiados, o simplemente emocionales.Usted puede tener las mejores ideas del mundo, pero si no puede comunicarlas por escrito, nadie va a poder hacer nada con sus ideas fantásticas. Por otro lado, ideas comunes que han sido escritas y expresadas correctamente, son más probables de llamar la atención. La manera en la cual usted decide escribir tiene que ver con la acceptación del público.

COLOQUIALISMOS

Coloquialismos son palabras y frases informales como *a lot, in a bind, pulled it off,* y otras parecidas. Estas palabras y frases son ampliamente usadas en conversaciones entre amigos, pero en la comunicación por escrito, éstas mismas denotan una actitud descuidada o de una proximidad que puede hacer que su mensaje no sea tomado muy en serio. Incluso, puede parecer que está insultando al lector, sin que ésta sea su intención. Un amistoso tono coloquial es aceptable en una carta personal; de todos modos, un tono más formal es mejor en las comunicaciones de negocios, ya que estos se leen e interpretan más seriamente. Compare los siguientes párrafos. Si usted recibiera uno de estos dos comunicados, ¿cuál de ellos lo recibiría con más seriedad?

I think the way we promote people around here stinks. People who aren't that good at their jobs get promoted just because they pal around with the right people. That puts across the idea that it doesn't matter how much time I put in at work or how good of a job I do; I won't get promoted unless I kiss up to the boss. I'm not that kind of guy.

I think our promotion system is unfair. Average and below average employees receive promotions simply because they befriend their superiors. This practice leaves the impression that commitment and quality of work are not considered. I choose not to socialize with my supervisors, and I feel as though I am not being promoted for that reason alone.

El autor del primer párrafo suena como si no tomase su trabajo muy seriamente. Y, seguramente no es así; pero éste no ha logrado comunicarse seriamente por escrito porque usó un lenguaje que es más apropiado para sus amigos y no para su supervisor. El autor del segundo párrafo, comunica su seriedad usando un lenguaje más formal. Este último logra hacerlo sin la necesidad de sonar muy inteligente. Él usa un lenguaje directo y simple pero no coloquial.

Las siguientes oraciones demuestran la diferencia entre la dicción formal y la coloquial. Al sustituir las palabras marcadas en negrilla, la oración se transforma en una más formal en lugar de coloquial.

Coloquial	Más palabras formales
I have around three hours to finish this job.	I have **about** three hours to finish this task.
The pasta was real good.	The pasta was **very** good.
We got sick from the food.	We **became ill** from the food.
It looks like we could win.	It looks **as if** we could win.
I'm awful tired.	I'm **very** (or **quite** or **extremely**) tired.

TONO

Tono describe la actitud emocional del autor hacia el lector o la audiencia. Mientras más razonable y efectivo sea el mensaje, es más probable que sea considerado serio. Emociones furiosas muy raramente convencen a alguien que cambien de opinión, y muy raramente convencen a alguien que está indeciso. La persuasión requiere la presentación lógica de argumentos claros. Un lector u oyente dará más credibilidad a un argumento que parezca justo y objetivo. La emoción puede reducir la credibilidad. Úsela cuidadosamente.

EVITE EL ENOJO

Evite las palabras acusadoras o enojadas que hacen demandas. Consideren los dos parágrafos que siguen. ¿Cuál de ellos es más probable que convenza al lector a tomar un tipo de acción?

I just got this stupid credit card bill in the mail. None of these outrageous charges are mine. I can't believe some big corporation like yours can't find a way to keep its records straight or keep its customers from being cheated. If you can't do any better than that, why don't you just give it up? I reported my stolen credit card five days before any of these charges were made, and yet you idiots have charged me for these purchases. The fine print you guys are so fond of putting in all of your contracts says I am not (I'll say it again just to help you understand) **not** responsible for these charges. I want them removed immediately.

The credit card bill I received on April 25 contains several charges that need to be removed. I reported my stolen credit card on April 20. When I called to make the report, the representative referred me to the original contract that states, "No charges in excess of $50.00 nor any made more than 24 hours after the card has been reported stolen shall be charged to the customer's account." Naturally, I was quite relieved. All of the charges on this account were made more than 24 hours after I reported the stolen card. Please remove the charges from my account. Thank you very much.

No importa cuán enojado usted se encuentre, el dar a su lector cierta credibilidad no es sólo una cortesía, sino que puede tener mejores resultados. (Este principio es más importante si usted está escribiendo a su supervisor, empleado, o a un cliente que cuando escribe a una gran compañía de crédito). La primera carta es la que usted escribe sin revisar, inmediatamente después de haber leído su cuenta de crédito. Incluso el escribir esa primera carta le puede ayudar a desahogarse. El destruirla le puede hacer sentir inclusive mejor. Yá después, se puede sentar a escribir la carta que va a enviar—la segunda versión.

Use muy cuidadosamente el *sarcasmo* (lenguaje de insulto) y la *ironía* (decir lo opuesto de lo que realmente quiere decir"). Así como la rabia, el sarcasmo pone en duda su credibilidad. El uso excesivo del sarcasmo puede hacerlo parecer infantil o ridículo en vez de razonable y lógico. Además, para que la ironía sea efectiva, el lector tiene que reconocerla de inmediato. A no ser que el lector entienda completamente su mensaje, usted se arriesga de que éste confunda o distorcione su mensaje. Una frase irónica o sarcástica puede envigorar su escritura, pero requiere mucha precisión y práctica en su uso.

EVITE LO BONITO

Evite el uso de palabras que hacen que su escritura suene exhuberante o bonita. Pese a que la escritura pueda parecer entretenida al lector, quizás no se la tome seriamente. El párrafo que sigue protesta una decisión, pero falla en explicar por qué la desición estaba incorrecta. Puede que llame la atención del lector, pero no producirá resultado ninguno, menos, quizás la despedida del autor.

I'm just a li'l ol' girl, but it's clear to me that this decision is dead wrong. I'm afraid that the people who made it have a serious intelligence problem. If they took their two IQ points and rubbed them together, they probably couldn't start gasoline on fire. If you were one of those people…. Oh well, it's been nice working for you.

La conclusión implícita en las última oración del autor—el hecho de que ella no espera trabajar aquí por mucho tiempo—es probablemente cierto.

EVITE LA POMPOSIDAD

Evite palabras que hacen que su escritura suene pomposa o cermoniosa. Muy poca gente responde positivamente a un tono condecendiente o patronizador. Compare los dos párrafos que siguen, ambos escritos por empleados que buscan una promoción. ¿A cuál de los dos empleados promovería usted si es que ambos estuvieran compitiendo por la misma posición y ambos tuvieran las mismas calificaciones?

If you examine my service and work record for the past two years, I believe you will find a dedicated, hard-working employee who is ideal for the floor manager position. I believe all employees should be on time for their jobs. You will see that my attendance record is impeccable, no absences and no tardies. You can see from my monthly evaluations that I was a high-quality employee when I was hired and that I have consistently maintained my high standards. I strive to be the kind of employee all managers wish to hire, and I believe my record shows this. I am also extremely responsible. Again, my record will reflect that my supervisors have confidence in me and assign additional responsibility readily to me because I am someone who can handle it. I am a man of my word, and believe that responsibility is something to be treasured, not shirked. As you compare me with other employees, I feel confident that you will find I am the most competent person available.

Thank you for considering me for the position of floor manager. As you make your decision, I would like to highlight three items from my service and work record. First, in two years I have not missed work and have been tardy only once, as the result of an accident. Second, my supervisors have given me the highest ratings on each of the monthly evaluations. Finally, I was pleased to have been given additional responsibilities during my supervisors' vacation times, and I learned a great deal about managing sales and accounts as a result. I welcome the challenge that would come with a promotion. Thank you again for your consideration.

Ambos empleados hacen resaltar algunos de los aspectos de sus trabajos previos. Pero el primer empleado se siente muy seguro que sus superiores se pongan a pensar de que si él realmente tiene la habilidad de ser un buen supervisor. Nadie quisiera trabajar para un supervisor que se inclina por declarar que "la responsabilidad es algo que se debe valorar y no criticar." El acercamiento del otro lector está dispuesto a hacer una mejor impresión en aquellos que basarán las decisiones.

EVITE LAS EMOCIONES BARATAS

Evite el lenguaje que está lleno de sentimentalismo o emociones baratas. Se arriesga a que su lector se burle. El siguiente párrafo muestra este gran error.

> We were so deeply hurt by your cruel thoughtlessness in failing to introduce us to Charlton Heston. He is the most wonderful, talented, masculine actor to have ever walked the face of the earth. My friend Charlotte and I so admire him and have ever since we can remember. Our admiration is a deep-channeled river that will never stop flowing. I'm sure you can imagine just how sorely disappointed and deeply wounded we were when we were not given the opportunity and honor to shake the hand and hear the voice of this great man. Neither I nor my dearest friend can seem to forget this slight, and I'm sure we will remain scarred for many years to come.

¡Qué nauseabundo! En lugar de arrepentirse de no haber presentado el autor al gran actor Charlton Heston, el lector seguramente se felicita a sí mismo de no haber permitido que este loco se aproximara a él.

PUNTO DE VISTA CONSISTENTES

Muchos autores pueden escribir desde el punto de vista de la primera persona (*I, me, we, us, my, our*), de la segunda persona (*you, your*), o de la tercera persona (*she, he, one, they, her, him, them, hers, his, one's, theirs*). Evite el cambio de puntos de vista dentro o entre oraciones. Mantenga el punto de vista consistente.

Inconsistente	Consistente
Citizens pay taxes, which entitles them [third person] to have some say in how their [third person] government is run. We [first person] have a right to insist on efficient use of our tax dollars.	We citizens pay taxes, which entitles us to have some say in how our government is run. We have a right to insist on efficient use of our tax dollars.
I [first person] enjoyed my trip to the park. You [second person] could see trees budding, flowers blooming, and baby animals running all over.	I enjoyed my trip to the park. I saw trees budding, flowers blooming, and baby animals running all over.

PARALELISMO

Dos o más ideas equivalentes que tienen el mismo propósito dentro de una oración, tienen que ser presentadas en la misma forma. Esto se conoce como estructura paralela. El uso de oraciones de estructuras paralelas no sólo ayuda a que su composición sea clara y comprensible, pero también ayuda al lector a reconocer rápidamente ideas muy similares. Vea el siguiente ejemplo de ideas, frases, y cláusulas paralelas.

No Paralelo	Paralelo
My roommate is miserly, sloppy, and a bore.	My roommate is miserly, sloppy, and boring. My roommate is a miser, a slob, and a bore.
My vacuum cleaner squealed loudly, shook violently, and dust filled the air.	My vacuum cleaner squealed loudly, shook violently, and filled the air with dust.
We soon discovered that our plane tickets were invalid, that our cruise reservations had never been made, and our travel agent left town.	We soon discovered that our plane tickets were invalid, that our cruise reservations had never been made, and that our travel agent had left town.

Los pares de ideas deben ser siempre presentados en construcción paralela. Las siguientes oraciones presentan dos o más ideas equivalentes que usan formas similares.

The committee finds no original and inspiring ideas in your proposal. What is original is not inspiring, and what is inspiring is not original.

We came, we saw, we conquered.

Belle was a timid, talented, and creative person.

Ask not what your country can do for you; ask what you can do for your country.

USANDO UN LENGUAJE NEUTRO

Puede parecer que el lenguaje es neutro, simplemente una herramienta para expresar ideas. A pesar de que esto es parcialmente verdadero, el lenguaje refleja nuestros valores y comunica a otros las diferencias sexuales y otros temas más. Si una cultura tiene sus dudas sobre las diferencias sexuales, el lenguaje inmediatamente llega a ser un vehículo para expresar y quizás perpetuar esas diferencias. Uno de los primeros pasos para combatir dichos prejuicios, es examinar el lenguaje y cambiarlo de una manera que ya no refleje y por consiguiente perpetue los estereotipos sexuales.

Algunas personas se resisten a cambiar el lenguaje, pensando en que las palabras son inofensivas y que aquéllos que se sienten ofendidos, simplemente son muy sensibles. El hecho está en que muchos lectores son sensibles y se ofenden por el uso tradicional de los pronombres masculinos al dirigirse a ambos sexos. Por ejemplo: *"Man must fulfill his destiny"* o *"Emily Dickinson was a great poetess"* que reflejan un arcaísmo o un insulto.

Cuando palabras cargadas emocionalmente, distraen al lector, el mensaje sufre. Un lector que se ofende por las palabras no logrará obtener el significado.

TRAMPAS DE GÉNERO

A continuación le presentamos unos ejemplos del tipo de lenguaje que tiene que evitar ya que su carga emocional puede distorcionar las ideas.

Nombre y Pronombres Personales

La dificultad más grande se encuentra en el uso de pronombres. Si el pronombre *he* es usado para referirse a un número indefinido de personas—profesor, estudiante, o servicio de correos"—la suposición inmediata parece

Pobremente Escrito	Mejor Escrito
A presidential candidate must realize that his life is no longer his own.	Presidential candidates must realize that their lives are not their own
If a student wishes to change his schedule, he must see his advisor, who will tell him how to proceed.	a) If a student wishes to change his or her schedule, he or she must see his or her advisor, who will tell him or her how to proceed. [Esta oración resuelve el problema de la concordancia al usar ambos pronombres singulars; el femenino y el masculine. De todas formas la composición parece ser extraña e inconvincente.] b) If students wish to change their schedule, they must see their advisor, who will tell them how to proceed. [En esta oración, al convertir el nombre *student* en su plural *students* resuelve el problema de la concordancia de pronombres.] c) If you wish to change your schedule, see your advisor, who will tell you how to proceed. [Esta oración usa el segundo pronombre personal "you" y "your."]
If anyone wants to improve his test scores, he should take good notes and study.	a) Anyone who wants improved test scores should take good notes and study. [Re-estructure la oración para evitar la referencia pronominal.] b) Students who want to improve their test scores should take good notes and study. [Convierta *anyone* en el plural *students*.] c) Anyone who wants to improve his or her test scores should take good notes and study. [Use ambos pronombres singulares, el masculine y el femenino.]

ser que todos los profesores, estudiandes y carteros son masculinos. El problema se presenta de nuevo cuando se tiene una lista de palabras como (*someone*, *somebody*, *everyone*, *no one*, o *nobody*). A continuación hay algunos ejemplos de las trampas de género y la manera de revisarlas.

Note que simplemente no puede cambiar las palabras *he* y *she* por *they* y *theirs*. Está gramáticamente incorrecto. Los pronombres *they* y *their* no concuerdan con su antecedente, *anyone*, en número ya que *anyone* es singular y *they* es plural.

La mujer como subordinada del hombre

Hay muchas maneras delicadas en que los escritores siempre hacen ver a la mujer como subordinada del hombre.

Pobremente Escrito	Mejor Escrito
A principal and his staff need to establish good communication.	The principal and staff need to establish good communication.
If you ask the nurse, she will summon the doctor if he is available.	If you ask, a nurse will summon an available doctor.
Bob took his wife and children to a movie.	Bob and Mary took their children to a movie.
Emil asked his secretary to check the mail.	Emil asked the secretary to check the mail.

Muchos escritores caen en la misma trampa cuando se refieren a hombres de acuerdo con sus abilidades, mientras que se refieren a las mujeres de acuerdo con su belleza o apariencia.

Pobremente Escrito	Pobremente Escrito
Dr. Routmeir and his attractive, blond wife arrived at the party at 9:00 P.M.	a) Dr. and Ms. Routmeir arrived at the party at 9:00 P.M. b) Herman and Betty Routmeir arrived at the party at 9:00 P.M.
The talented violinist and his beautiful accompanist took the stage.	The violinist and the accompanist took the stage.

Note que en las dos primeras oraciones de la primera columna, se refiere al hombre por su profesión, mientras que se refiere a la mujer por su apariencia. Para evitar el asignar valores opuestos, al hombre por su apariencia y a la mujer por sus logros, refiérase a ambos en el mismo contexto, ya sea profesional o físico. En el primer ejemplo hace mención del hombre por su título, y la mujer no es identificada menos como una extensión de él, perteneciente al hombre. Para evitar este tipo de error refiérase a ambos por sus nombres.

Trabajo de hombres, trabajo de mujeres

Evite hacer referencias sobre género o sexo especialmente cuando se trata de trabajos hechos tradicionalmente por hombre o mujeres—esas tradiciones ya no estan en práctica. La primera oración que sigue hace indagaciones tradicionales, mientras que la segunda no.

> When a man on board collapsed, a lady pilot emerged from the cockpit, and a male nurse offered assistance.
> When a passenger collapsed, a pilot emerged from the cockpit, and a nurse offered assistance.

Las referencias *lady pilot* y *male nurse* llaman la atención a sí mismas porque asumen que el lector automáticamente va a asignar un género para el trabajo. Los lectores que no piensan en terminos de los estéreotipos tradicionales, estaran ofendidos por las ideas del escritor que se ha involucrado en ideas estereotípicas.

EVITANDO TRAMPAS DE GENERO

Como escritor usted tiene que darse cuenta del efecto que tienen estas referencias de género en los lectores. Usted puede evitar ofender a sus lectores usando un lenguaje específico de género en tres maneras: use términos neutros, use el plural, o estructure de nuevo sus oraciones de manera que no hagan referencia a las distincciones de género. Todas estas tácticas han sido ilustradas en las oraciones revisadas anteriormente. Más ejemplos a continuación.

Use términos de género neutros

En inglés existen muchas palabras que tradicionalmente han tomado formas diferentes para personas del género masculine y femenino. Más y más estas distincciones se han vuelto obsoletas. En estos días, más y más gente prefiere referirse a ambos hombres y mujeres en sus funciones particulares. Estos cambios no tienen que ser extraños como podrá ver en la tabla que sigue a continuación.

Uso específico de genero	Género neutro
waiter, waitress	server
stewardess, steward	flight attendant
policeman, policewoman	police officer
chairwoman, chairman	chairperson, chair
man-made	synthetic, artificial
foreman	supervisor
manpower	employees, personnel
man, mankind	humanity, people

En el pasado era muy común el uso de la plabra hombre para referirse a toda la humanidad, ambos hombres y mujeres. Hoy día, ese tipo de uso puede ofender a mucha gente. La oración que sigue demuestra este tipo de uso mientras que la segunda ofrece una alternativa más apropiada.

If man wishes to improve his environment, he must improve himself.

If humanity wishes to improve its environment, each individual must improve.

Convertir al plural

Uno de los problemas más dificultosos de resolver es cómo usar una oración como, "A student must do his homework if he wants to succeed in his classes." La manera más fácil de evadir el problemático *he* es convertir los pronombres singulares *he, she, him, hers,* o *his* en el pronombre plural *they* y *their*. Claro que naturalmente, usted tiene que revisar los antecedents de esos pronombres de manera que estos también sean plurales (vea la Lección 13). "*Students must do their homework if they want to succeed in their classes.*" Estos son otros ejemplos.

Uso específico de genero	Género neutro
The doctor uses his best judgment.	Doctors use their best judgment.
Every student must do his homework.	Students must do their homework.
A company executive is wise to choose his words carefully.	Company executives are wise to choose their words carefully.
If a manager wants respect, he should behave respectably.	Managers who want respect should behave respectably.

Estructure de nuevo oraciones para evitar referencias de género

Finalmente, usted puede evitar completamente referencias de género al estructurar otra vez sus oraciones. Vea como se hace esto en los ejemplos que siguen.

Uso específico de genero	Género neutro
Man has always turned to his intellect to solve problems.	People have always turned to their intellect to solve problems.
A company executive is wise to drive himself relentlessly.	Anyone who desires success must work relentlessly.
A nurse must take her job seriously.	A nurse must take the job seriously.
Someone left his umbrella in the cloakroom. He should call Lost and Found.	The person who left an umbrella in the cloakroom should call Lost and Found.
The ladies enjoyed the shopping trip.	The shoppers enjoyed their trip.

Técnicas de aprendizaje

Ponga mucha atención al tono y estilo de todo lo que lee y escribe. ¿Es el nivel de formalidad apropiado en el mensaje y para la audiencia? ¿Siente que hay un uso exagerado de emoción? ¿Es el punto de vista consistente? ¿Están las ideas equivalentes presentadas igualmente? ¿Existen en la escritura referencias de género? ¿Si es así, cree usted que van a ofender al lector?

L·E·C·C·I·Ó·N

COMMUNICANDO SUS IDEAS

20

RESUMEN DE LA LECCIÓN

La lección anterior se trataba de las palabras y las oraciones. Esta lección final se trata de los temas generales relacionados con una composición. Al enfocarse en el propósito de su escritura, usted puede desarrollar sus ideas de una manera lógica y efectiva para que de esta manera pueda impactar a sus lectores.

El saber usar los detalles del lenguaje es muy importante, pero el propósito principal de una composición es comunicar a su audiencia un mensaje con una idea específica. La mayor parte de las composiciones hacen una de las tres cosas: informan, explican, o presentan un argumento. Escribir efectivamente ocasiona el descubrir lo que usted quiere decir, organizar sus ideas, y presentar las de la forma más lógica y efectiva. Esta lección cubre todos estos aspectos.

ESCRIBIR PARA INFORMAR

Una buena y organizada composición, es clara, simple, y ordenada. En los negocios es importante ser directo en cuanto a la escritura. Nadie tiene tiempo de leer introducciones largas, es decir las palabras que usted escribió como introducción. Los mejores tipos de comunicación son aquellos que presentan el asunto directa y claramente.

De todas manera, el empezar es muy difícil. Al hacerse preguntas a sí mismo usted podrá aclarar sus ideas y ser más directo.

1. En una sóla oración, haga un resumen de la idea principal de su mensaje. Si usted hace esto el resto le será más fácil. Si es posible, presente esta idea de la manera más clara y simple. Si su composición presenta una lista de información, hechos, o estadísticas, trate de resumir el propósito de su información. La oración debe contestar la respuesta: ¿Porqué estoy escribiendo esto?

2. Seguidamente, piense en sus lectores. ¿Quién leerá lo que escribe? ¿Cuál es su relación con sus lectores: superior, colegas, clients? Pensar en sus lectores o su audiencia le ayuda a usar un tono o actitud apropiada.

3. En un borrador anote todas las ideas que le vienen a la cabeza, es decir, toda la información que crea necesaria incluir en su composición. Esto puede ser hecho en una lista o en una hoja de papel con palabras e ilustraciones conectadas por líneas; use el método que mejor funcione para usted. Ponga toda la información por escrito y donde sean accesibles.

4. Una vez que la información ya esté reunida, piense en las maneras en que puede organizarla. Piense en su mensaje como un flujo de ideas, uno cuyas partes están conectadas. ¿Cómo puede uno organizar la información de tal manera que la conección se vea fácil y natural? Considere estas reglas de organización:

   - **Orden espacial:** el orden en el cual los elementos son organizados, uno en relación con otro
   - **Orden cronológico:** orden de tiempo
   - **Orden lógico:** comience con la premisa más básica, siga con lo que se puede derivar de esta premisa
   - **General a lo específico:** comience con una declaración general, llegue a un hecho específico
   - **Específico a general:** de una serie de hechos específicos, llegue a una generalización

5. Ahora es hora de empezar a escribir. Comience con una oración o un párrafo corto que indica el propósito de su composición, revise lo que aprendió en el primer paso para estar seguro de sus puntos principales.

6. Desarrolle en un solo párrafo, cada una de las ideas que identificó en los pasos 3 y 4. Si las ideas secundarias pueden ser presentadas efectivamente tanto en una forma de lista como dentro de las oraciones, use una lista similar a la anterior para hacer resaltar sus propósitos originales. Sea fiel a una idea en cada párrafo y, si es possible, mantenga los párrafos cortos y concisos.

Si usted está escribiendo para negocios, use listas enumeradas o con puntos como se hizo en esta página. Trate de lograr una presentación lógica y clara, una que está bien organizada y libre de palabras execivas que no dicen nada. He aquí un mapa del proceso de organización de un escritor en repuesta a un pedido: la planificación, la organización, la idea principal, la audiencia, y el comunicado completo.

La Planificación

Idea Principal: Mr. Lundsky requested information about the printers (models, date of purchase) used in our department and justification for the technology requests we made last year.

Propósito: Provide the information so the department can get what it requested

Audiencia: Mr. Lundsky, technology coordinator

I. Data
   A. Current computers and memory
      1. PS1, 4 mb RAM
      2. PS2, 8 mb RAM
      3. AST, 8 mb RAM
      4. PS2, 8 mb RAM
      5. Compaq Presario, 16 mb RAM
   B. Printers
      1. NEC, 1991
      2. Epson, 1992
      3. HP Laserjet II, 1993
      4. HP Deskjet 560, 1995

II. Requests
   A. Additional printer
      1. HP Deskjet 660C for Compaq Presario
      2. Reason: newest, most powerful computer needs color capability
   B. Memory upgrades
      1. two 8 mb SIMMs for PS1
      2. two 8 mb SIMMs for PS2s respectively
      3. 8 mb SIMMs for AST
   C. Justification for memory upgrades
      1. Most recent programs require a minimum of 16 mb RAM
      2. 8 mb SIMMs are the most cost effective

The Memo

To: Mr. Lundsky

From: Allie McGinnis

Re: Technology assessment and needs of sociology department as requested

Date: May 9, 1996

I am providing the information you requested about equipment we have in our department. I am also outlining our additional requests and the reasons for these requests.

These are the machines, memory capacity, and printers we have at this time:

- PS1, 4 mb RAM, NEC Silentwriter printer (purchased in 1991)
- PS2, 8 mb RAM, Epson LQ2 dot matrix printer (both purchased in 1992)
- AST, 8 mb RAM, no printer (purchased in 1992)
- PS2, 8 mb RAM, Laserjet II printer (both purchased in 1993)
- Compaq Presario, 16 mb RAM, HP Deskjet 560 (purchased 1995)

We are requesting five 8-megabyte memory SIMMs to upgrade all of the computers to at least 16 mb of RAM. The most recent programs we have purchased require a minimum of 10 mb. Eight-mb SIMMS are the most cost-effective way to buy additional memory. A single 8-mb SIMMs is $95.00, while 4-mb SIMMs are $72.00 and 2-mb SIMMs are $59.00 each. We also need an HP Deskjet 660C. We plan to move the HP Deskjet 560 to the AST, which has no printer, and put the new printer with color capability on our newest, most powerful unit.

Thank you for considering our request.

ESCRIBIR PARA EXPLICAR

Otra forma de composición que posiblemente use muy a menudo es la explicación. Quizá tenga que dar las razones de una acción o reglamento, o quizá tenga que explicar cómo es un producto.

Para este tipo de composición, siga el mismo proceso de planeamiento que se sigue para presentar una información.

1. Haga un resumen de la idea o el propósito principal.

2. Determine quiénes son su audiencia, sus lectores.

3. Anote en un borrador las ideas que le vienen a la cabeza.

4. Organice sus ideas.

5. Comience por establecer el propósito.

6. Desarrolle sus ideas en párrafos.

Mientras escribe, mantenga estas sugerencias en mente.

- Presente los pasos en un orden lógico. El orden cronológico es es más apropiado para este proceso.
- Asegúrese de haber explicado clara, exacta, y detalladamente cada paso para que el lector pueda seguir y entender.
- Use hechos y ejemplos para apoyar cada una de sus puntos.
- Ponga atención especial a la introducción y a la conclusion. Estos dos párrafos son la base para entender su composición, y dan al lector una idea de la información que usted está presentando. Haga que estos dos párrafos funcionen a su favor.

Este es un ejemplo real: la planificación que hizo un escritor antes de escribir el borrador de una carta a un cliente para explicarle cómo operar una nueva máquina fotocopiadora.

Idea princial: explain to new customer how to use a new copy machine
Audiencia: members of promotional staff at KCBD-TV, all of whom use the copier
Propósitos: (1) clearly explain use, (2) clearly outline maintenance procedures, (3) provide basic trouble-shooting suggestions, (4) assure them that the copier is reliable and that service is quick, should they need it.

   I. Daily use
      A. Copying
      B. Enlarging/reducing
      C. Handling multiple-page documents
  II. Maintenance
      A. Routine
         1. Loading paper
         2. Adding toner
         3. Clearing paper jams
      B. Troubleshooting
         1. Electrical problems
         2. Paper jams
         3. Failure to copy
      C. Calling the technician
         1. Business day number
         2. Emergency service

III. Reliability
  A. Warranties
  B. Weekly maintenance checks
  C. Service
  D. Two-hour replacement guarantee

Primer párrafo: Everyone in the promotional department at KCBD-TV will find this new Sharp copy machine a huge improvement over the older model. You'll appreciate how easy it is to use this new copier for daily tasks, and anyone can perform the routine maintenance on the machine. This, our most reliable copier, is backed by a long-term warranty and a quick, efficient service plan.

ESCIBIR PARA PERSUADIR

Otro de los estilos de composición más comunes se relaciona con presentar un argumento claro y convencedor. Su comunicación escrita puede ser un solo mensaje o puede que sea uno de los primeros de una serie que con el tiempo llegue a ser un compromiso. Cada tipo de argumento requiere un acercamiento diferente; de todas maneras, ambos tipos de comunicación persuasiva tienen que tener tres características comunes: orden lógico, base sólida, y credibilidad.

ORDEN LÓGICO

Incluso las mejores y más brillantes ideas no tendrán un impacto si el lector no puede reconocer o seguirlas. Argumentos tienen que ser cuidadosamente organizados para crear el efecto que se desea con el lector.

Las posiciones más fuertes están al comienzo y al final de cualquier tipo de comunicación. Ponga sus argumentos más fuertes en uno de ellos, y ordene el resto de una manera que puedan ser presentados clara y fácilmente.

SOPORTE SÓLIDO

Una buena persuasión no solamente hace un reclamo claro y fuerte sino provee una base sólida. Éstas son algunas maneras de apoyar sus declaraciones:

- **Ejemplos**, ya sean personales o investigados.
- **Evidencia objetiva**, como hechos y estadísticas.
- **Citas y autoridad**. Use una autoridad calificada y contemporánea y cuyas opiniones sean aplicables a su situación especial. Si el lector no está familiarizado con la autoridad que usted menciona, explique porque esa persona está calificada para serlo.
- **Analogía**. Si puede pensar en una clara comparación con la cual el lector pueda estar familiarizado, preséntela claramente. Cuidadosamente señale todas las similitudes y explique por qué la comparación es beneficiosa y aplicable.

Si usted apoya un hecho moral o emocional, use declaraciones lógicas o emocionales hechas con descripciónes vivas.

CREDIBILIDAD

Un comunicado escrito es *creíble* si el lector cree en el escritor o lo encuentra confiable. Sin importar la historia entre el escritor y el lector, cada mensaje provee una nueva oportunidad para establecer credibilidad.

En cualquier tipo de mensaje, usted puede establecer credibilidad de una de estas tres maneras:

- **Demuestre su conocimiento del tema.** Demuestre que usted tiene experiencia personal que hace que su perspectiva del tema sea confiable. Si usted no tiene experiencia personal que puede usar, demuestre que ha consultado una variedad de fuentes confiables y neutrales, y que sus ideas estén basadas en su investigación.
- **Demuestre equidad y objetividad.** Pruebe que ha tomado en consideración todos los puntos de vista significicantes. Tiene que convencer al lector que entiende y valora otras opiniones sobre el tema, y que además los valora. Muestre que ha considerado cuidadosamente toda la evidencia, incluso áquella que no apoya su punto de vista.
- **Busque áreas de acuerdo.** Esto es de mucho valor si su mensaje es el comienzo de un proceso que resultará en un acuerdo. Determine que tienen en común los diferentes puntos de vista y comience a desarrollar credibilidad y confianza en una base común.

Use los mismos seis pasos señalados anteriormente para planear una mensaje persuasivo. Examine el siguiente plan de un autor con un mensaje escrito a favor de un nuevo reglamento de horarios.

Queja: store needs a better system for scheduling employees

Audiencia: store's general manager

Propósito: (1) point out problems inherent in the current policy, (2) outline the qualities a new scheduling policy should have, (3) point out the advantages of a scheduling policy with those qualities, (4) show that customers will receive better service, (5) show that employees understand and are willing to share the burden of developing and implementing a new policy.

   I. Problems with current policy
     A. Based solely upon seniority
     B. Arbitrary within seniority brackets
     C. Equal number for all shifts
       1. Doesn't allow for employees willing to be flexible
       2. Not enough employees during peak sales times
       3. Too many employees during off-peak sales times
       4. Leads to minimal employee commitment
     D. No incentive for good attendance
   II. Qualities of an effective scheduling policy
     A. Continues to take seniority into account

   B.   Allows for individual preferences

   C.   Allows for flex time

   D.   Allows for increased numbers during peak times, reduced numbers during off times

   E.   Provides an incentive for reliable attendance

   F.   Provides an incentive to work least desirable hours

III.   Advantages of a policy with these characteristics

   A.   Improved customer service

      1.   Better service during peak times

      2.   Quality service during off-peak times

   B.   Less absenteeism

   C.   Improved employee morale

   D.   Sense of ownership among employees

IV.   Development and implementation

   A.   Management responsibilities

   B.   Employee responsibilities

      1.   Committee willing to develop plan during unpaid time

      2.   Willing to assume some responsibility for implementation

Primer párrafo: Since we value customer service, our store needs to develop a scheduling system that will provide better customer service while at the same time fostering an increased sense of commitment among employees.

Siempre y cuando escriba, mantenga en mente que tiene que presentar un mensaje tan claro y simple como le sea possible. Escriba para expresar no para impresionar. Las palabras deben comunicar el mensaje, y no interferir con éste.

Técnicas de aprendizaje

Escriba un comunicado pidiendo un aumento de sueldo. Si usted puede hacer eso, se dará cuenta que el tiempo invertido en este libro ha sido de mucho beneficio. ¡Vaya, atrévase! Lo peor que puede pasar es que: Quiensea que lea el comunicado va a hablar o escribir negándole su pedido. Incluso si esto pasa, su composición habrá hecho una impresión. Si usted presentó unos cuantos y buenos argumentos, pueden que éstos se queden en la mente de su supervisor, incluso si no obtiene el aumento de sueldo. El próximo llegará tan pronto como si nunca hubiese escrito el comunicado. El mejor resultado de esto: Obtiene su aumento de sueldo. ¿Cómo puede usted perder? Incluso si usted no envia el comunicado, escríbalo. Le ayudará a tener más confianza en sí mismo, y puede ser que lo envie en un tiempo más oportuno. Puede pensarlo, revisarlo, añadir algo y luego enviarlo.

Siempre que tenga una idea y quiere que lo tomen seriamente, escriba un comunicado. No pasará mucho tiempo en que la gente comience a darse cuenta de que usted tiene el poder de la pluma. Una palabra de advertencia: Muchas personas son intimidadas por otras que pueden escribir. Use términos más suaves cuando les escriba, y escríbales con más frecuencia. Transcurrido el tiempo apreciarán sus ideas y su habilidad.

PRUEBA FINAL

Ahora que usted ha invertido bastante tiempo en mejorar su habilidad de gramática y escritura, tome esta prueba final para ver cuánto ha aprendido. Si tomó el examen de evaluación al comienzo del libro, tiene una buena manera de comparar lo que usted sabía en ese entonces y lo que sabe ahora.

Cuando termine esta prueba, corríjala y compare su puntaje con el puntaje de la prueba de evaluación. Si el puntaje de ahora es más alto que el de entonces, felicidades—se ha beneficiado bastante de su duro trabajo. Si su puntaje muestra poco mejoramiento, quizá hay algunas lecciones que tenga que repasar. ¿Nota un patrón en el tipo de preguntas que contestó mal? Cualquiera que sea su puntaje en esta prueba final, mantenga este libro a mano para revisar y usarlo como referencia cuando no esté seguro de cómo usar algunas reglas gramaticales.

En la siguiente página, hay una hoja de respuestas que puede usar para llenar las respuestas correctas. O, si usted prefiere, simplemente encierre en un círculo las respuestas en este libro. Si el libro no le pertenece, escriba los números del 1-50, en una hoja de papel aparte y escriba sus respuestas en la misma. Tome el tiempo que sea necesario para terminar esta pequeña prueba. Cuando termine, compare sus respuestas con las de la página de respuestas que sigue a este examen. Cada respuesta le dice cuál lección de este libro le enseña las reglas gramaticales de la pregunta.

1. ⓐ ⓑ ⓒ ⓓ
2. ⓐ ⓑ ⓒ ⓓ
3. ⓐ ⓑ ⓒ ⓓ
4. ⓐ ⓑ ⓒ ⓓ
5. ⓐ ⓑ ⓒ ⓓ
6. ⓐ ⓑ ⓒ ⓓ
7. ⓐ ⓑ ⓒ ⓓ
8. ⓐ ⓑ ⓒ ⓓ
9. ⓐ ⓑ ⓒ ⓓ
10. ⓐ ⓑ ⓒ ⓓ
11. ⓐ ⓑ ⓒ ⓓ
12. ⓐ ⓑ ⓒ ⓓ
13. ⓐ ⓑ ⓒ ⓓ
14. ⓐ ⓑ ⓒ ⓓ
15. ⓐ ⓑ ⓒ ⓓ
16. ⓐ ⓑ ⓒ ⓓ
17. ⓐ ⓑ ⓒ ⓓ
18. ⓐ ⓑ ⓒ ⓓ
19. ⓐ ⓑ ⓒ ⓓ
20. ⓐ ⓑ ⓒ ⓓ

21. ⓐ ⓑ ⓒ ⓓ
22. ⓐ ⓑ ⓒ ⓓ
23. ⓐ ⓑ ⓒ ⓓ
24. ⓐ ⓑ ⓒ ⓓ
25. ⓐ ⓑ ⓒ ⓓ
26. ⓐ ⓑ ⓒ ⓓ
27. ⓐ ⓑ ⓒ ⓓ
28. ⓐ ⓑ ⓒ ⓓ
29. ⓐ ⓑ ⓒ ⓓ
30. ⓐ ⓑ ⓒ ⓓ
31. ⓐ ⓑ ⓒ ⓓ
32. ⓐ ⓑ ⓒ ⓓ
33. ⓐ ⓑ ⓒ ⓓ
34. ⓐ ⓑ ⓒ ⓓ
35. ⓐ ⓑ ⓒ ⓓ
36. ⓐ ⓑ ⓒ ⓓ
37. ⓐ ⓑ ⓒ ⓓ
38. ⓐ ⓑ ⓒ ⓓ
39. ⓐ ⓑ ⓒ ⓓ
40. ⓐ ⓑ ⓒ ⓓ

41. ⓐ ⓑ ⓒ ⓓ
42. ⓐ ⓑ ⓒ ⓓ
43. ⓐ ⓑ ⓒ ⓓ
44. ⓐ ⓑ ⓒ ⓓ
45. ⓐ ⓑ ⓒ ⓓ
46. ⓐ ⓑ ⓒ ⓓ
47. ⓐ ⓑ ⓒ ⓓ
48. ⓐ ⓑ ⓒ ⓓ
49. ⓐ ⓑ ⓒ ⓓ
50. ⓐ ⓑ ⓒ ⓓ

PRUEBA FINAL

1. Which of the following is a sentence fragment (not a complete sentence)?
   a. Property taxes rose by three percent.
   b. Although the mayor and three members of the city council were defeated.
   c. The voters were decidedly against building the new stadium.
   d. Be sure to vote in the next election.

2. Which version is correctly capitalized?
   a. After we headed west on interstate 70, my uncle Paul informed us that his Ford Taurus was almost out of gas.
   b. After we headed west on Interstate 70, my Uncle Paul informed us that his Ford Taurus was almost out of gas.
   c. After we headed West on Interstate 70, my Uncle Paul informed us that his Ford Taurus was almost out of gas.
   d. After we headed West on interstate 70, my Uncle Paul informed us that his Ford taurus was almost out of gas.

3. Which version is punctuated correctly?
   a. That building, with the copper dome is our state capitol.
   b. That building with the copper dome, is our state capitol.
   c. That building, with the copper dome, is our state capitol.
   d. That building with the copper dome is our state capitol.

4. Which version is punctuated correctly?
   a. The temperature was eighty degrees at noon; by 6:00 P.M. it had dropped to below forty.
   b. The temperature was eighty degrees at noon, by 6:00 P.M. it had dropped to below forty.
   c. The temperature was eighty degrees at noon by 6:00 P.M., it had dropped to below forty.
   d. The temperature was eighty degrees at noon by 6:00 P.M. it had dropped to below forty.

5. Which version is punctuated correctly?
   a. It was one managers' idea to give us a month's vacation.
   b. It was one manager's idea to give us a months vacation.
   c. It was one manager's idea to give us a month's vacation.
   d. It was one managers idea to give us a month's vacation.

6. Which version is punctuated correctly?
   a. "Look out! shouted Jake. There's a deer in the road."
   b. "Look out!" shouted Jake. "There's a deer in the road."
   c. "Look out"! shouted Jake. "There's a deer in the road."
   d. "Look out! shouted Jake." "There's a deer in the road."

7. Which version uses parentheses correctly?

   a. On the first trip my family took to the amusement park (I was only five years old at the time), I got lost in an area known as Adventureland.

   b. On the first trip (my family took to the amusement park) I was only five years old at the time, I got lost in an area known as Adventureland.

   c. On the first trip my family took to the amusement park I was only five years old at the time, (I got lost in an area known as Adventureland).

   d. On the first trip my family took to the amusement park I was (only five years old) at the time, I got lost in an area known as Adventureland.

8. Choose the subject that agrees with the verb in the following sentence.

   _____ of the musicians have arrived at the concert.

   a. Each

   b. Neither

   c. One

   d. Two

9. Which of the following sentences is most clearly and correctly written?

   a. Bart told us all about the fish he caught while waiting in line at the movie theater.

   b. At the movie theater, Bart told us about the fish he caught while we waited in line.

   c. As we waited in line at the movie theater, Bart told us about the fish he caught.

   d. As we waited in line, Bart told us about the fish he caught at the movie theater.

10. Which version is in the active voice?

   a. The president of the P.T.A. requested donations for the new auditorium.

   b. For the new auditorium, donations had been requested by the P.T.A. president.

   c. Donations for the new auditorium were requested by the president of the P.T.A.

   d. Donations were requested by the P.T.A. president for the new auditorium.

11. Which version has a consistent point of view?

   a. Last Sunday, we went canoeing on the Platte River. You could see bald eagles high in the trees above us.

   b. While we were canoeing last Sunday on the Platte River, high in the trees above us, you could see bald eagles.

   c. We went canoeing last Sunday on the Platte River, and high in the trees above us, we could see bald eagles.

   d. High in the trees above, the bald eagles were looking down at you, as we canoed on the Platte River last Sunday.

12. Which version uses punctuation correctly?

   a. Yikes! Did you see that mouse run under the stove.

   b. Yikes! Did you see that mouse run under the stove?

   c. Yikes? Did you see that mouse run under the stove!

   d. Yikes: Did you see that mouse run under the stove?

13. Which of the underlined words in the following sentence should be capitalized?

My <u>sister</u> has been studying <u>biology</u> at the <u>university</u> of Maryland since last <u>fall</u>.

  a. Sister
  b. Biology
  c. University
  d. Fall

Para las respuestas 14 y 15, elija la forma correcta del verbo.

14. When he was asked to select a pair of mittens, Danny _____ the blue ones.
  a. has chosen
  b. choosed
  c. choose
  d. chose

15. The snow _____ to fall late yesterday afternoon.
  a. began
  b. begun
  c. had began
  d. begins

16. Which version is most clearly and correctly written?
  a. Jeff told Nathan that his car battery was dead.
  b. When Jeff spoke to Nathan, he said his car battery was dead.
  c. Jeff told Nathan about his dead car battery.
  d. Jeff told Nathan that the battery in Nathan's car was dead.

Para las respuestas 17–19, elija la opción que completa correctamente la oración.

17. The cat _____ in a patch of sun on the front porch.
  a. is laying
  b. is lying
  c. lays
  d. laid

18. When I heard the unusual sound, I _____ walked through the house and searched each room very _____.
  a. calmly, carefully
  b. calmly, careful
  c. calm, careful
  d. calm, carefully

19. I have _____ idea how these _____ got in my sweater.
  a. know, wholes
  b. know, holes
  c. no, holes
  d. no, wholes

20. Which of the following sentences contains a redundancy, that is, it repeats words that express the same idea?
  a. Del shouted as loudly as he could, but no one heard him.
  b. Twenty minutes had passed before the fire trucks arrived.
  c. Yesterday, the senator made the same speech at three different locations.
  d. For a wide variety of different reasons, more people are using computers.

21. Which version has a parallel structure?

a. He is a man of many talents. He repairs small machines, he cooks gourmet meals, and you should see his lilies and orchids.

b. He is a man of many talents. There's a talent for repairing small machines, he cooks gourmet meals, and then there are the lilies and orchids.

c. He is a man of many talents. He repairs small machines, he cooks gourmet meals, and he grows lilies and orchids.

d. He is a man of many talents: repairing small machines, cooking gourmet meals, and he grows lilies and orchids.

22. Which of the following sentences contains a cliché?

a. Looking for Harriet's ring was like searching for a needle in a haystack.

b. The reason I can't have lunch with you is because I have a dentist appointment.

c. The crooked fence looked like a row of teeth in need of braces.

d. As costs go up, so do prices.

23. Which version uses periods correctly?

a. A. J. Sullivan and Dr Henry Harris will return to the U.S. tomorrow at 4 PM.

b. A. J. Sullivan and Dr. Henry Harris will return to the U.S. tomorrow at 4 P.M.

c. A. J. Sullivan and Dr. Henry Harris will return to the US tomorrow at 4 P.M.

d. A J Sullivan and Dr Henry Harris will return to the U.S. tomorrow at 4 PM.

24. Which version is correctly capitalized?

a. Many Meteorologists are predicting that the West will have the wettest winter on record.

b. Many meteorologists are predicting that the west will have the wettest winter on record.

c. Many Meteorologists are predicting that the West will have the wettest Winter on record.

d. Many meteorologists are predicting that the West will have the wettest winter on record.

25. Three of the following sentences are faulty. They are either run-ons or comma splices. Which one is NOT a faulty sentence?

a. A group of lions is called a pride a group of elephants is called a herd.

b. Josh told me he would meet us at the zoo at noon, he never showed up.

c. We waited three hours, finally, Karen decided to give him a call.

d. A young sheep is known as a lamb, but a young goat is known as a kid.

26. Which version is punctuated correctly?

a. There are many differences—aside from the obvious ones—between a ten-year-old and an adolescent.

b. There are many differences: aside from the obvious ones—between a ten-year-old and an adolescent.

c. There are many differences—aside from the obvious ones, between a ten-year-old and an adolescent.

d. There are many differences aside from the obvious ones—between a ten-year-old and an adolescent.

27. Which is the correct punctuation for the under-lined portion?

The explosion broke several windows in the <u>factory however</u> no one was injured.

a. factory, however
b. factory however;
c. factory; however,
d. factory, however;

28. Which version uses hyphens correctly?
a. My soft-spoken brother-in-law did not raise his voice when he saw that his car had been damaged in the parking-lot.
b. My soft spoken brother-in-law did not raise his voice when he saw that his car had been damaged in the parking-lot.
c. My soft-spoken brother-in-law did not raise his voice when he saw that his car had been damaged in the parking lot.
d. My soft-spoken brother in-law did not raise his voice when he saw that his car had been damaged in the parking lot.

29. Which version is punctuated correctly?
a. Ms. Jeffers who is my physics teacher, coaches the girls' basketball team.
b. Ms. Jeffers, who is my physics teacher, coaches the girls' basketball team.
c. Ms. Jeffers who is my physics teacher coaches the girls' basketball team.
d. Ms. Jeffers who, is my physics teacher, coaches the girls' basketball team.

Para las respuestas 30–34, elija la opción que completa correctamente la oración.

30. Several manuals, each with detailed instruc-tions, _____ with your new computer.
a. were sent
b. was sent
c. has been sent
d. sent

31. Jessica and _____ are looking in the grass for one of her earrings; _____ will be hard to find.
a. me, it
b. me, they
c. I, they
d. I, it

32. Yesterday, I _____ my watch on this table, but now _____ gone.
a. set, it's
b. set, its
c. sat, its
d. sat, it's

33. I took Jane's _____ and did not _____ the job.
a. advice, except
b. advice, accept
c. advise, accept
d. advise, except

34. Raul _____ attending the meetings because he had _____ many other commitments.
a. quite, too
b. quite, to
c. quit, to
d. quit, too

35. Which version is punctuated correctly?
   a.   The recreation center will show the follow-ing movies: *Charlotte's Web, Jungle Book,* and *Annie,* the cost will be $2.50 per ticket.
   b.   The recreation center will show the follow-ing movies; *Charlotte's Web, Jungle Book,* and *Annie;* the cost will be $2.50 per ticket.
   c.   The recreation center will show the follow-ing movies: *Charlotte's Web, Jungle Book,* and *Annie.* The cost will be $2.50 per ticket.
   d.   The recreation center will show the follow-ing movies—*Charlotte's Web, Jungle Book,* and *Annie.* The cost will be $2.50 per ticket.

36. Which version is punctuated correctly?
   a.   Disappointed by his loss in the tennis match Andrew stomped off the court.
   b.   Disappointed by his loss in the tennis match, Andrew, stomped off the court.
   c.   Disappointed by his loss in the tennis match, Andrew stomped off the court.
   d.   Disappointed by his loss in the tennis match Andrew stomped, off the court.

37. Which version is punctuated correctly?
   a.   The woman who lives across the street was born on July 4, 1922, in Washington, D.C.
   b.   The woman, who lives across the street, was born on July 4, 1922, in Washington, D.C.
   c.   The woman who lives across the street, was born on July 4, 1922 in Washington, D.C.
   d.   The woman who lives across the street was born on July 4, 1922 in Washington D.C.

Para la pregunta 38, elija la correcta conjugación del verbo.

38. By next fall, I _____ to all fifty of the United States.
   a.   would be
   b.   should have been
   c.   will have been
   d.   had been

39. Three of the following sentences are punctuated correctly. Which one is punctuated INCOR-RECTLY?
   a.   My son's baseball game was postponed; it was raining too hard.
   b.   Because it was raining too hard; my son's baseball game was postponed.
   c.   My son's baseball game was postponed because it was raining too hard.
   d.   It was raining too hard, and my son's base-ball game was postponed.

40. Which of the following should NOT be hyphen-ated?
   a.   one-fifteen in the morning
   b.   the sixteenth-president of the United States
   c.   a thirty-second commercial
   d.   a thousand-dollar profit

41. In which of the following sentences is the under-lined verb NOT in agreement with the subject of the sentence?
   a.   Why <u>are</u> the books on your shelf always arranged this way?
   b.   There <u>is</u> only one more person waiting in line.
   c.   Here <u>are</u> the sunglasses you ordered.
   d.   What <u>is</u> the reasons for your late arrival?

42. In which of the following sentences is the under-lined pronoun INCORRECT?

   a. The teacher who won the award was <u>her</u>.

   b. <u>He and I</u> plan to visit you tomorrow.

   c. When can <u>she</u> come over for dinner?

   d. Both Michael and Steven will finish <u>their</u> homework early.

43. Which version is punctuated correctly?

   a. The hospital doesn't have Rebeccas' records.

   b. The hospital does'nt have Rebecca's records.

   c. The hospital doesn't have Rebecca's records'.

   d. The hospital docsn't have Rebecca's records.

44. Which version is written correctly?

   a. <u>Cheers</u> was one of the most popular shows ever on television.

   b. *Cheers* was one of the most popular shows ever on television.

   c. "Cheers" was one of the most popular shows ever on television.

   d. CHEERS was one of the most popular shows ever on television.

45. Which of the following sentences is in the passive voice?

   a. Every morning this week, Zeke brought bagels to work.

   b. Each day, he selected several different kinds.

   c. Generally, more than half of the bagels were eaten before 9:00.

   d. We've asked him to stop because we've all gained a few pounds.

46. We noticed the _____ of his cologne when he _____ in front of us.

   a. scent, past

   b. scent, passed

   c. sent, passed

   d. sent, past

47. Ian is the _____ of the triplets, but _____ all the members of his family, he is the only one with a talent for music.

   a. smallest, among

   b. smallest, between

   c. smaller, between

   d. smaller, among

48. _____ the person _____ found my wallet.

   a. Your, who

   b. Your, which

   c. You're, that

   d. You're, who

49. I _____ you thought he would be much older _____ I am.

   a. supposed, then

   b. suppose, then

   c. suppose, than

   d. supposed, than

50. Evan doesn't like chocolate; he _____ away his _____ of cake.

   a. through, piece

   b. through, peace

   c. threw, peace

   d. threw, piece

RESPUESTAS

Si usted no contestó con la respuesta correcta, puede encontrar ayuda para ese tipo de en la lección indicada a la derecha de la pregunta.

1. b.	Lección 3	
2. b.	Lección 1	
3. d.	Lección 4	
4. a.	Lección 5	
5. c.	Lección 7	
6. b.	Lección 8	
7. a.	Lección 9	
8. d.	Lección 12	
9. c.	Lección 15	
10. a.	Lección 11	
11. c.	Lección 19	
12. b.	Lección 2	
13. c.	Lección 1	
14. d.	Lección 10	
15. a.	Lección 10	
16. d.	Lección 13	
17. b.	Lección 14	
18. a.	Lección 15	
19. c.	Lección 17	
20. d.	Lección 18	
21. c.	Lección 19	
22. a.	Lección 18	
23. b.	Lección 2	
24. d.	Lección 1	
25. d.	Lección 3	

26. a.	Lección 7
27. c.	Lección 6
28. c.	Lección 9
29. b.	Lección 4
30. a.	Lección 12
31. d.	Lección 13
32. a.	Lección 14
33. b.	Lección 17
34. d.	Lección 16
35. c.	Lección 6
36. c.	Lección 4
37. a.	Lección 5
38. c.	Lección 10
39. b.	Lección 6
40. b.	Lección 9
41. d.	Lección 12
42. a.	Lección 13
43. d.	Lección 7
44. c.	Lección 8
45. c.	Lección 11
46. b.	Lección 16
47. a.	Lección 15
48. d.	Lección 14
49. c.	Lección 17
50. d.	Lección 16

A · P · É · N · D · I · C · E

PREPARÁNDOSE PARA UN EXAMEN ESTANDARD

La mayoría de nosotros nos ponemos nerviosos al tomar un éxamen, especialmente si estos son estandarizados, es decir, en los cuales nuestros puntajes pueden tener un significado impactante en nuestros futuros. La nervosidad es natural e incluso puede ser beneficiosa si uno aprende a canalizarla correctamente en energía positiva.

Las siguientes páginas proven sugerencias para sobrepasar la ansiedad de tomar un examen tanto en los días y semanas antes del examen como durante el mismo.

DOS O TRES MESES ANTES DEL EXAMEN

El mejor método de combatir la ansiedad de un examen es estar preparado. Eso significa dos cosas: saber lo que se espera ver en el examen y revisar el material y las técnicas que serán examinadas.

SEPA QUE ESPERAR

¿Qué conocimiento o habilidad seran examinados en la prueba? ¿Qué es lo que se espera que usted sepa? ¿Qué habilidades está usted supuesto a demostrar? ¿Cuál es el formato de la prueba? ¿De alternativa multiple, falso o verdadero, ensayo? Si es posible vaya a la biblioteca o a la librería y obtenga una guía de estudio que le demuestre con un ejemplo como será el éxamen. O quizás, la agencia que está administrando la prueba para que usted obtenga un trabajo, provee guías de estudio o conduce secciones de tutoría. Mientras más sepa que esperar, más confidente se sentirá para responder las preguntas.

REVISE EL MATERIAL Y LAS HABILIDADES EN LAS QUE USTED SERÁ EXAMINADO

El hecho de que usted esté leyendo este libro significa que ya ha tomado los pasos necesarios en relación a lectura y comprensión. Ahora, ¿hay otros pasos que usted necesita tomar? ¿Hay otras areas temáticas que usted necesita revisar? ¿Puede hacer más mejoras en esta u otra area? Si realmente usted está nervioso o si es que ha pasado mucho tiempo desde la última vez que usted reviso el material, se sugiere que quizás es major que compre una nueva guía de estudio, tome una clase en su vecindario o trabaje con un tutor.

Mientras más sabe usted lo que se espera en el examen y mientras más confidente se siente usted con el material o las habilidades a ser evaluadas menos ansioso se sentirá y hará major en el examen.

LOS DÍAS ANTES DEL EXAMEN

REVISE, NO ESTUDIE A LA RÁPIDA

Si usted ha estado preparandose y revisando el material durante las semanas antes del éxamen, no hay necesidad de que se desespere días antes de tomarlo. Es muy probable que el estudiar a la rápida lo confunda y le haga sentir nervioso. En lugar de eso, establesca un horario para revisar relajadamente todo lo que usted ha aprendido.

ACTIVIDAD FÍSICA

Haga ejercicios antes del día del éxamen. Al hacerlo enviará más oxígeno a su cerebro y permitirá que su función de razonamiento increse en el día que tome el examen. Aquí, moderación es la palabra clave. Usted no quiere hacer muchos ejercicios para que después se sienta totalmente exhausto, pero un poco de actividad física dará vigor a su cuerpo y cerebro. Caminar es un ejercicio muy bueno, de bajo impacto y promotor de energía.

DIETA BALANCEADA

Como su cuerpo, su cerebro para funcionar necesita los nutrientes apropiados. Antes del día del examen coma fruta y vegetales en abundancia. Comidas que sean altas en contenido de lecitin, como por ejemplo pescado y habichuelas que son buenas selecciones. Lecitin es una proteína su cerebro necesita para optimizar su actividad. Incluso, semanas antes del examen, usted puede considerar una visita a su farmacia local para comprar una botella de lecitin en tabletas.

DESCANSO

Duerma bien antes de tomar el examen. Pero, no se exceda o quedará un tanto adormitado que es como si estubiese cansado. Baya a dormir a una hora razonable, lo suficientemente temprano como para tener unas cuantas horas que le permitan funcionar efectivamente. Usted se sentirá relajado y descansado si usted puede dormir bien durante los días previos al día del examen.

MARCHA DE ENSAYO

Cualquier momento antes de tomar el examen, haga una marcha de ensayo al lugar donde se va a llevar a cabo el examen para ver cuanto tiempo le toma llegar allá. El apresurarse incrementa su energía emocional y rebaja su capasidad intelectual, entonces, usted tiene que darse tiempo suficiente para llegar al lugar donde se administrará el examen. Llegar diez o quince minutos antes le da tiempo suficiente para calmarse y ubicarse.

MOTIVACIÓN

Para después del examen, planee algo así como una celebración—con su familia y amigos o simplemente usted solo. Asegúrese que va a ser algo esperado y que le va a gustar. Si usted tiene algo que realmente espera después de tomar el éxamen, usted podrá prepararse y avanzar más facilmente durante el examen.

EL DÍA DEL ÉXAMEN

Finalmente ha llegado el gran día esperado, el día del examen. Ponga su alarma lo suficientemente temprano para darse el tiempo necesario que requiere llegar al ludar donde el examen tomará lugar. Tome un buen desayuno. Evite todo lo que tenga un alto contenido de azucar, como por ejemplo donuts. Si bien una sobre-dosis de azucar hace que uno se sienta alerta y despierto, ésto solo dura por una hora más o menos. Cereal y tostadas, o algo que contenga en alto contenido de carbohidratos es la mejor opción. Coma en moderación. No debe tomar el examen con el estómago muy lleno ya que su cuerpo en lugar de canalizar todas las energías a su cerebro, las canalizará a su estómago.

Enpaque entre sus cosas un bocado alto en contenido energético para que así, si es que hay un descanso intermedio durante el examen, usted pueda comer algo. Bananas son lo mejor ya que tienen un contenido moderado de azucar y suficientes nutrientes cerebrales como por ejemplo, potasio. La mayor parte de los procuradores de examenes no dejan que uno coma cuando uno está tomando el examen, pero un dulce de menta no es un gran problema. Los dulces de menta son como sales aromáticas para el cerebro. Si usted pierde su concentración o sufre de una momentánea perdida de memoria, un dulce de menta le puede poner otra vez en forma. No se olvide de la anterior recomendación sobre el relajarse y tomar unos cuantos suspiros profundos.

Salga lo suficientemente temprano para así tener el tiempo suficiente de llegar al lugar del examen. Dese unos cuantos minutos extras por si hay un execivo tráfico. Cuando llegue, ubique el servicio y úselo. No muchas cosas interfieren con la concentración como el tener una vejiga llena. Seguidamente encuentre su asiento y asegúrese de que esté cómodo. Si no es así, dígaselo al procurador y trate de encontrar en lugar más adecuado.

Ahora relájese, y piense positivamente. Antes de que pueda darse cuenta, el examen terminará y usted saldrá de éste sabiendo que ha hecho un buen trabajo.

COMO DOMINAR LA ANSIEDAD DE UN EXAMEN

Bueno, usted sabe el material incluido en el examen. Usted ha revisado los temas y practicado las técnicas que serán evaluadas. Entonces, ¿porqué sigue sintiendo cosquilleos en el estómago?, ¿porqué tiene las palmas sudorosas y las manos temblorosas?

Incluso los más brillantes, mejor preparados examinantes a veces sufren de ataques de ansiedad antes de una prueba. Pero no se preocupe, usted puede sobrepasarlo. A continuación una lista de estrategias que le pueden ser útiles.

TOME EL EXAMEN RESPONDIENDO PREGUNTA POR PREGUNTA

Toda su atención debe de estar enfocada en la pregunta que está contestando. Borre de su mente pensamientos relacionados con preguntas ya contestadas o elimine preocupaciones de lo que viene después. Ponga toda su concentración donde le sea más beneficioso, en la pregunta que actualmente está contestando.

ADQUIERA UNA ACTITUD POSITIVA

Recuerdese a sí mismo que usted está preparado. A propósito si usted leyó este libro o algún otro de la serie del Learning Express, probablemente usted esté mejor preparado que la mayor parte de aquellos que estan tomando el examen. Recuerde que es solo una prueba y que usted tratará de hacerlo lo mejor posible. Eso es todo lo que se puede pedir de usted. Si esa voz de sargento dentro de su cabeza comienza a enviarle mensajes negativos, combátalos con sus propios mensajes positivos. Dígase a sí mismo:

- "Lo estoy haciendo bastante bien."
- "Estoy preparado para este examen."
- "Yo sé exactamente lo que tengo que hacer."
- "Yo sé que puedo obtener el puntaje que deseo."

Usted se puede imaginar. Recuerde de reemplazar mensajes negativos con sus propios mensajes positivos.

SI USTED PIERDE SU CONCENTRACIÓN

No se preocupe mucho. Es normal. Durante un examen largo, le pasa a todo el mundo. Cuando la mente está muy tensa o cansada, quieralo usted o no, ésta toma un descanso. Es fácil el volver a concentrarse si es que usted se da cuenta de que la ha perdido y que necesita tomar un descanso. Su cerebro necesita muy poco tiempo para descansar (a veces es questión de segundos).

Ponga de lado su lápiz y cierre los ojos. Respire profundo, y exhale muy lentamente. Escuche el sonido de su respiración mientras repite este ejercicio dos o más veces. Los pocos segundos que esto toma es el tiempo necesario que su cerebro necesita para relajarse y alistarse para poder enfocarse nuevamente. Este ejercicio también le ayudará a controlar los latidos de su corazón para así poder mantener la ansiedad al margen.

SI USTED SE LLEGA A PARALIZAR

No se preocupe por una pregunta que le hace tropezar incluso si usted sabe su respuesta. Márquela y siga adelante con la siguiente pregunta. Usted puede regresar a la pregunta más tarde. Trate de ponerla completamente de lado hasta que pueda regresar a ella. Deje que su subconciente trabaje en esa pregunta mientras que su conciencia se enfoca en otras cosas (una por una, naturalmente). Lo más probable es que este olvido pasajero pase cuando usted pueda volver a esa pregunta.

Si usted se paraliza antes de comenzar la prueba, esto es lo que tiene que hacer:

1. Haga ejercicios de respiración ya que le ayudarán a relajarse y enfocarse.
2. Recuerdese que usted está preparado.
3. Tome su tiempo para repasar el examen.
4. Lea algunas de las preguntas.
5. Decida cuáles son las más fáciles de contestar y comience por ellas.

Antes de nada usted estará listo.

ESTRATEGIAS PARA CONTROLAR EL TIEMPO

Uno de los elementos más importantes como también más horripilantes de un examen estandardizado es el tiempo. Ya que usted tendrá solamente un cierto número de minutos para cada sección, es muy importante que use sabiamente su tiempo.

MIDA SU VELOCIDAD

Una de las más importantes estrategías es el poder medir su velocidad. Antes de empesar, tome unos segundos para revisar el examen anotando siempre el número de preguntas y secciones que son más fáciles que el resto del examen. A continuación haga in horario estimado basándose en el tiempo que usted tenga para tomar el examen. Marque la parte central del examen y anote al lado de esta marca la hora que será cuando la mitad del tiempo del examen haya pasado.

SIGA ADELANTE

Una vez que haya comenzado a tomar el examen no pare. Si usted se dispone a trabajar lentamente con la idea de hacer menos errores, su mente se cansará y comensará a divagar. Entonces, usted terminará por hacer más errores porque no está concentrándose. Pero aún, si usted se toma mucho tiempo en responder las preguntas, terminará perdiendo el tiempo antes de que puede haber finalizado.

No pare si encuentra preguntas difíciles. Dejelas para más adelante y siga con las otras preguntas, usted puede regresar a ellas más tarde, si es que le queda tiempo suficiente. Una pregunta que le puede tomar en contestar más de cinco segundos, cuenta igual que otra que le puede tomar más tiempo en contestar. Entonces, elija primero las preguntas que tienen menos puntaje. Además que el contestar las preguntas fáciles primero le ayudarán a ganar más confidencia y a que se acondicione al examen. Quien sabe si a medida que toma el examen, usted encuentre información relacionada con aquellas preguntas más difíciles.

NO SE APRESURE

Siga avanzando, pero no se apresure. Piense que su mente es un cerrucho; en uno de sus lados está la energía emocional, y en el otro la energía intellectual. Cuando su energía emocional es alta, su capacidad intellectual es baja. Recuerde lo difícil que es razonar con alguien cuando usted se encuentra enojado. Por otra parte, cuando su energía intellectual está alta, su energía emocional es baja. El apresurarse eleva su energía emocional y reduce su capasidad intelectual. ¿Recuerda la última vez que llegó tarde al trabajo? Toda esa prisa causó que usted se olvidase de algo importante, como por ejemplo, su alnuerzo. Tome el examen rápidamente para que su mente no empiese a distraerse, pero no se apresure y termine agitado.

CONTRÓLESE A SÍ MISMO

Contrólese en la mitad del examen. Si usted está muy avanzado, usted sabe que está por buen camino, y que inclusive tendrá un poco de tiempo para revisar sus respuestas. Si usted está un tanto retrasado, usted tiene

las siguientes opciones: Usted puede incrementar la velocidad en que responde las preguntas, pero solo haga esto si es que usted se siente confortable con las preguntas, o puede usted saltar algunas preguntas para poder ganar algunos puntajes con las repuestas más fáciles. De todas maneras, esta estrategia tiene una desventaja, por ejemplo, si usted toma un examen donde tiene que marcar sus repuestas en círculos, si usted marca una pregunta correcta en el círculo incorrecto, sus preguntas serán evaluadas como malas. Ponga mucha atención en el número de pregunta si es que usted decide hacer eso.

EVITANDO LOS ERRORES

Cuando tome el examen usted quiere hacer los errores menos posibles. A continuación algunas tácticas para recordar.

CONTRÓLESE

¿Recuerde la analogía que se hizo de su mente con un cerrucho? Mantener baja su energía emocional y su capasidad intellectual alta, es la major manera de evitar hacer errores. Si usted se siente fatigado o preocupado, pare por unos cuantos segundos. Reconosca el problema (Ummm, siento un poco de presión en este momento), suspire profundamente un par de veces, y piense en algo positivo. Esto le ayudará a aliviar su ansiedad emocional e incrementará su capasidad intellectual.

DIRECCIONES

En muchos exámenes estandarizados, muchas veces un procurador lee las instrucciones en voz alta. Asegúrese de que usted entiende todo lo que se requiere en el examen. Si todo no está claro, pregunte. Escuche cuidadosamente las instrucciones para poder contestar las preguntas y asegúrese del tiempo que tiene para completar el exámen. Si es que no sabe cuanto tiempo va a durar el examen, escriba el tiempo de su duración en el examen. Si usted no tiene toda esta información importante, pregunte para obtenerla. Usted la necesita para poder rendir bien en el examen.

RESPUESTAS

Este consejo puede parecer un poco tonto pero es de mucha importancia. Coloque sus respuestas en los espacios en blanco o márquelas en los círculos correspondientes en la hoja de respuestas. Preguntas correctas en el lugar equivocado no tienen ningún valor, incluso le pueden quitar puntaje. Es una buena idea revisar cada cinco o diez preguntas para asegurarse que está en la sección correcta, de esta manera, si usted comete un error, no tiene que borrar por completo todo el examen.

LOS PASAJES DE LECTURA Y COMPRENSIÓN

Exámenes estandarizados muy a menudo ofrecen una sección diseñada para evaluar su capasidad de lectura y comprensión. La sección de lectura generalmente contiene pasajes de un párrafo o más. A continuación algunas tácticas para trabajar con estas secciones.

Esto puede sonar un tanto extraño, pero algunas preguntas se pueden contestar si haber elido el pasaje. Si el pasaje es corto (cuatro oraciones más o menos), lea las preguntas primero. Usted puede responder las preguntas usando el sentido común. Puede revisar sus respuestas más tarde, despues de que haya leido el pasaje. Sin embargo, si usted no está seguro no adivine; lea el pasaje cuidadosamente. Si usted no puede contestar ninguna de las preguntas, usted igual sabrá qué buscar cuando lea el pasaje. Esto focaliza su lectura y facilita que usted retenga información importante. Muchas de las preguntas se relacionan a detalles aislados del pasaje. Si de antemano usted sabe qué buscar, es más fácil encontrar la información.

Si una selección de lectura es larga y contiene más de diez preguntas, le tomará un tiempo el leer todas las preguntas primero. De todas maneras, tómese un par de segundos para revisar las preguntas y leer aquellas que son cortas. Seguidamente lea activamente el pasaje. Márquelo y si usted encuentra una oración que parece establecer la idea principal, subráyela. A medida que usted lea el resto del pasaje, enumere los puntos que apoyan la idea principal. Muchas preguntas se relacionarán a esa información. Si está subrayada o enumerada, usted puede localizarla facilmente. Otras preguntas pedirán información más detallada. Encierre en un círculo información referente a quién, qué, cuándo y dónde. Los círculos sera fácil de localizar si es que usted se encuentra con una pregunta que requiere información específica. Marcar un pasaje de esta manera, también ayuda a realizar su concentración y hace que muy probablemente usted vaya a recordar la información cuando se prepare a responder las preguntas del pasaje.

ELEGIR LAS RESPUESTAS CORRECTAS POR PROCESO DE ELIMINACIÓN

Asegúrese del contenido de la pregunta. Si usted no está seguro de lo que se está preguntando, nunca sabrá si ha elegido la respuesta correcta. Figure que es lo que la pregunta está indicando. Si la respuesta no es muy obvia, busque por señas en las otras opciones de preguntas. Note las similitudes y las diferencias en las selecciónes de repuestas. A veces, esto ayuda a ver la pregunta de una nueva perspectiva y facilita responderlas. Si usted no está seguro de la respuesta, use el proceso de eliminación. Primero, elimine cualquier possible respuesta que sea obviamente incorrecta. Luego estudie las demás posibilidades. Usted puede usar información relacionada que se encuentra en otras partes del exámen. Si usted no puede eliminar ninguna de las repuestas posibles, es mejor que salte la pregunta, continue con otra, y regrese a esta más tarde. Si usted todavía sigue teniendo el mismo problema de eliminación más tarde, adivine sus repuestas y continue tomando el exámen.

SI USTED ES PENALIZADO POR CONTESTAR RESPUESTAS INCORRECTAS

Antes del exámen, usted debe de saber si es que hay algun castigo por contestar con respuestas incorrectas. Si usted no está seguro, pregunte al procurador antes de que comience el exámen. Si es que usted puede adivinar o no, depende del castigo. Algunos exámenes estandardizados son evaluados de una manera tal que por cada respuesta incorrecta, se reduce el puntaje por un cuarto o la mitad de un punto. Cualquiera que sea la penalidad, si usted puede eliminar las suficientes opciones, para así lograr reducir la posibilidad de ser penalizado por contestar respuestas incorrectas, elimine las más que pueda.

Imaginemosnos que usted está tomando un examen en el cual cada pregunta tiene cuatro opciones y usted será penalizado por un cuarto de punto por cada respuesta equivocada. Si usted no tiene idea alguna y no puede eliminar ninguna de las preguntas, es mejor que deje la respuesta sin contestar, ya que la posibilidad de responder con la respuesta correcta es una de cada cuatro. Esto hace que la penalidad y la posibilidad sean iguales. De todas maneras, si usted puede eliminar una de las posibles respuestas, las posibilidades estan ahora en su favor. Usted tiene la opción de uno en tres de responder la pregunta correctamente. Afortunadamente, muy pocos exámenes son evaluados usando este sistema tan elaborado, pero si su examen es uno de ellos,

esté al tanto de las penalidades y calcule sus opciones antes de adivinar una pregunta.

SI USTED TERMINA TEMPRANO

Use cualquier tiempo que le queda al final del examen o al final de una sección para revisar su trabajo. Primero, asegúrese de que puso las respuestas en el lugar adecuado y mientras hace esto también asegúrese de que contestó cada pregunta una sola vez. Muchos de los exámenes estandardizados son evaluados de una manera en la cual preguntas con más de dos respuestas son marcadas como incorrectas. Si usted ha borrado una repuesta, asegúrese de que lo ha hecho bien. Observe por marcas o borrones que puedan interferir con la evaluación del mismo.

Después de haber revisado estos posibles errores, revise una vez más las preguntas más difíciles. Si bien quizás usted haya oido la creencia popular de que es mejor no cambiar una pregunta, no tome este consejo seriamente. Si usted tiene una buena razón para creer que una respuesta está incorrecta, cámbiela.

DESPUÉS DEL EXAMEN

Una vez que haya terminado, felicitece a sí mismo. Usted ha trabajado bastante para prepararse. Ahora es hora de que se relaje y entretenga. ¿Recuerda aquella celebración que planeó antes del examen? Ahora es tiempo de que la celebre.

¡BUENA SUERTE!